HOUGHTON MIFFLIN HARCOURT

Go Math!

Intensive Intervention

RtI **Response to Intervention Tier 3**

Skill Packs

Grade 4

www.hmhschool.com

Printed in the U.S.A.

ISBN 978-0-547-94511-8

6 7 8 9 10 0928 20 19 18 17 16 15 14 13

4500428776 ^ B C D E F G

Contents

Skills

1 Group and Count by Tens and Ones to 100 .... IIN1
2 Tens and Ones IIN3
3 Understand Place Value IIN5
4 Order on a Number Line IIN7
5 Addition Facts and Strategies IIN9
6 Practice Addition Facts IIN11
7 Practice Subtraction Facts IIN13
8 Model 2-Digit Addition IIN15
9 2-Digit Addition with Regrouping IIN17
10 Model 2-Digit Subtraction IIN19
11 Subtract 1-Digit from 2-Digit Numbers IIN21
12 2-Digit Subtraction with Regrouping IIN23
13 Skip-Count IIN25
14 Find a Number Pattern IIN27
15 Equal Groups IIN29
16 Relate Addition to Multiplication IIN31
17 Arrays IIN33
18 Multiply with 2 and 4 .... IIN35
19 Multiply with 2 and 5 .... IIN37
20 Multiply with 1 and 0 .... IIN39
21 Multiply with 4 .... IIN41
22 Multiply with 6 .... IIN43
23 Missing Factors IIN45
24 Multiplication Table IIN47
25 Multiplication Facts Through 10 .... IIN49
26 Multiplication Properties IIN51
27 Practice Multiplication Facts IIN53
28 Model Multiplication by 1-Digit Numbers IIN55

29 Round to the Nearest Ten IIN57
30 Round to the Nearest Hundred IIN59
31 Plane Figures IIN61
32 Sides and Vertices IIN63
33 Slides, Flips, and Turns IIN65
34 Congruent Figures IIN67
35 Symmetry IIN69
36 Solid Figures IIN71
37 Faces, Edges, Vertices IIN73
38 Use Arrays to Divide IIN75
39 Relate Division and Subtraction IIN77
40 Multiplication and Division Fact Families IIN79
41 Division Facts Through 5 .... IIN81
42 Part of a Whole IIN83
43 Part of a Group IIN85
44 Compare Fractions IIN87
45 Fractions Equal to 1 .... IIN89
46 Count Coins IIN91
47 One Dollar IIN93
48 Dollar and Cents IIN95
49 Time to the Hour IIN97
50 Time to the Half Hour IIN99
51 Time to the Quarter Hour IIN101
52 Read a Thermometer IIN103
53 Read Tables and Charts IIN105
54 Read a Tally Table IIN107
55 Read a Bar Graph IIN109
56 Make a List IIN111
57 Outcomes IIN113
58 Use a Customary Ruler IIN115

59	Measure to the Nearest Inch	IIN117
60	Ounces and Pounds	IIN119
61	Cups, Pints, Quarts, and Gallons	IIN121
62	Use a Metric Ruler	IIN123
63	Measure to the Nearest Centimeter	IIN125
64	Grams and Kilograms	IIN127
65	Milliliters and Liters	IIN129
66	Column Addition	IIN131
67	Perimeter	IIN133
68	Area	IIN135
69	Length, Width, and Height	IIN137
70	Explore Volume	IIN139

Name ____________________

Group and Count by Tens and Ones to 100

Skill 1

Vocabulary

tens
ones

Learn the Math

You can count tens and ones to find how many.

Circle groups of ten. Write how many tens and ones. Then write the number.

Step 1 Circle groups of ten.

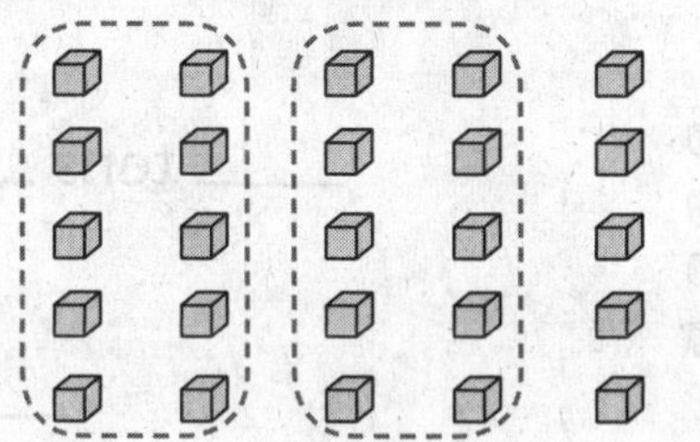

Step 2 Write how many tens.

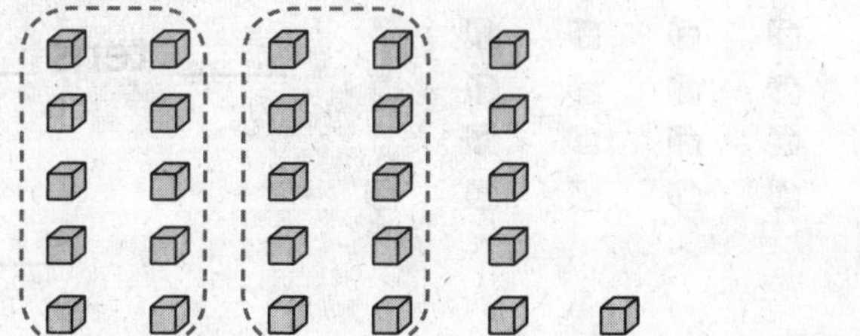

_______ tens

Step 3 Write how many ones.

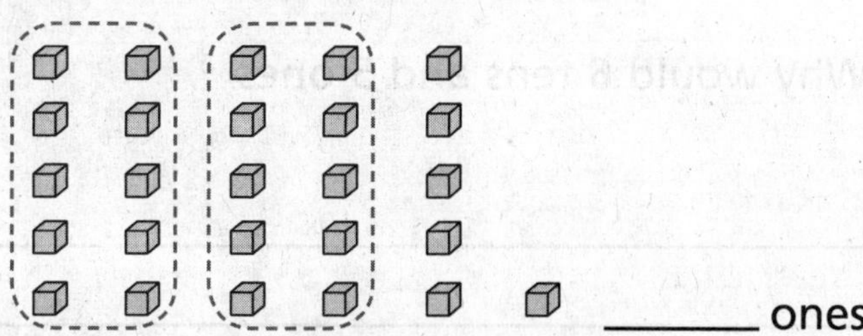

_______ ones

So, there are 2 tens and 6 ones, or _______.

Do the Math

Circle groups of tens. Write how many tens and ones. Then write the number.

1. 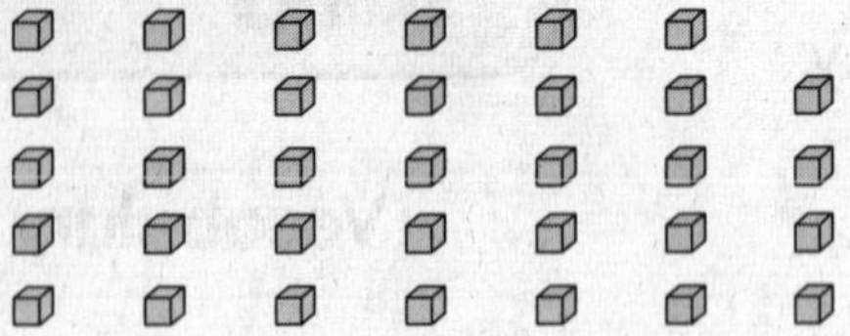 _____ tens _____ ones

_____

2. 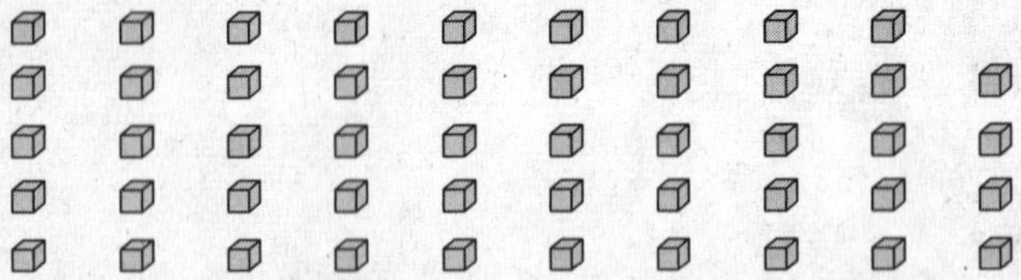 _____ tens _____ ones

_____

3. 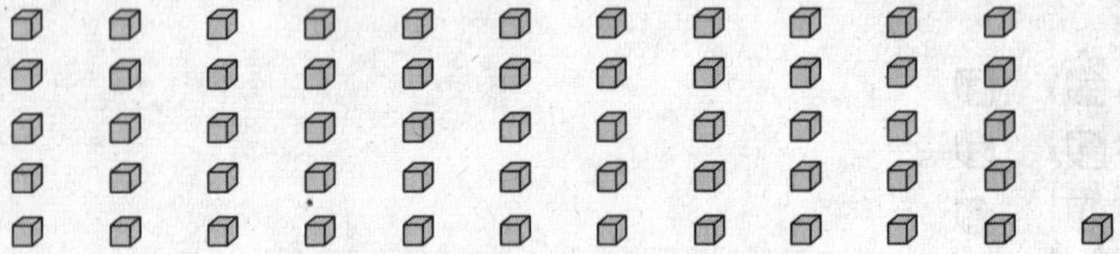 _____ tens _____ ones

_____

Check

4. Look back at Problem 3. Why would 6 tens and 5 ones be the wrong answer?

_____

_____

_____

_____

Name________________________________

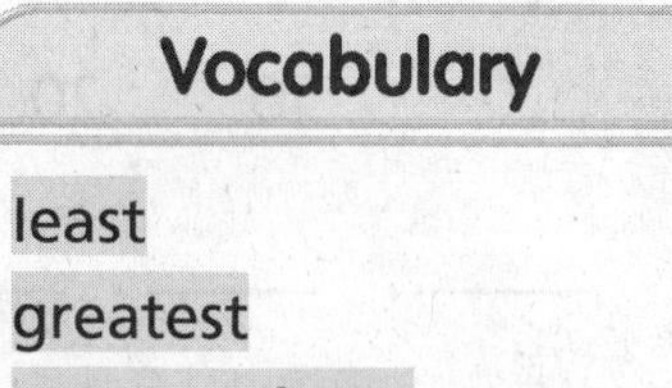

Learn the Math

You can use a number line to order numbers.

Vocabulary

least

greatest

number line

Order these numbers from least to greatest.

79 44 63

Step 1 Find the numbers on the number line.

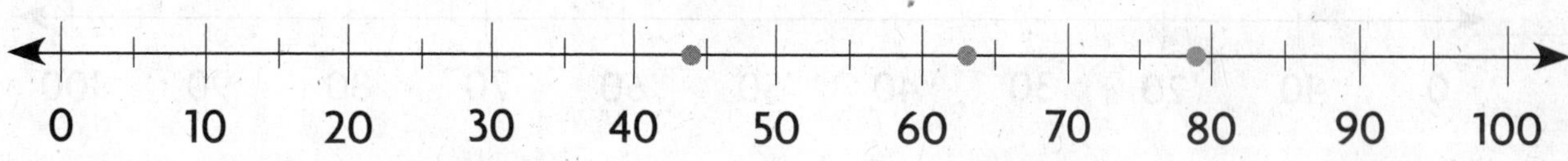

Step 2 Read the numbers from left to right.
Write them in that order.

44, ______, ______

Order the numbers from greatest to least.

58 82 21

Step 1 Find the numbers on the number line.

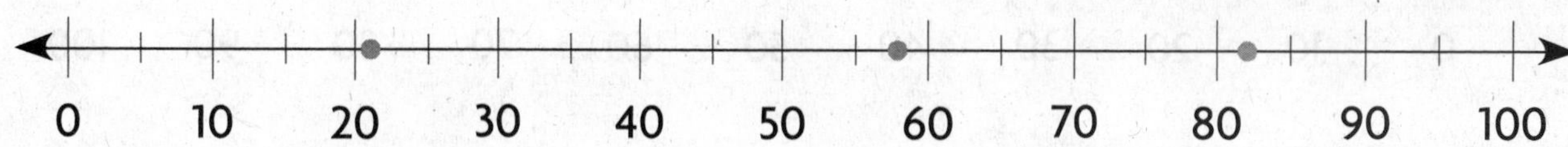

Step 2 Read the numbers from right to left.
Write them in that order.

82, ______, ______

Use the number line. Write the numbers in order from least to greatest.

1. 37 29 54

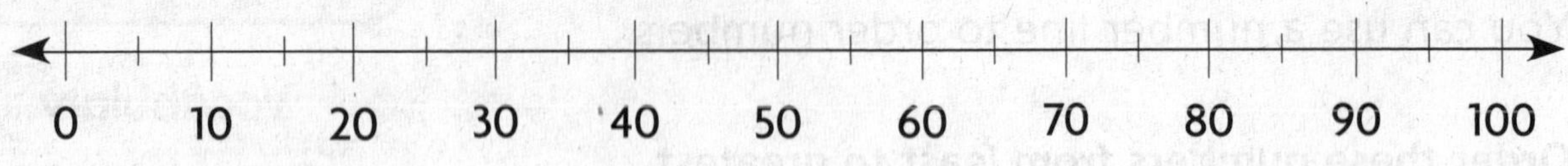

_____, _____, _____

2. 42 70 64 97

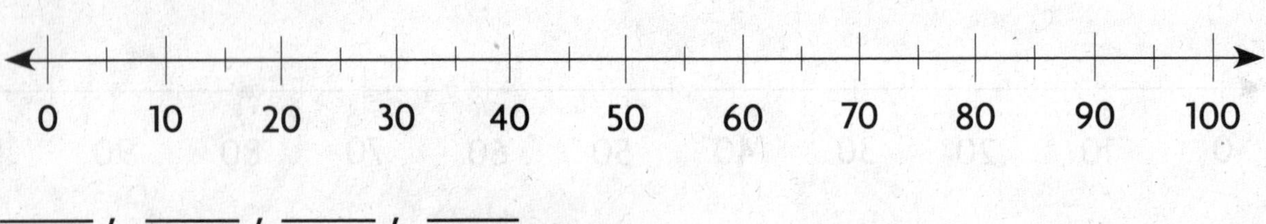

_____, _____, _____, _____

Use the number line. Write the numbers in order from greatest to least.

3. 26 14 43

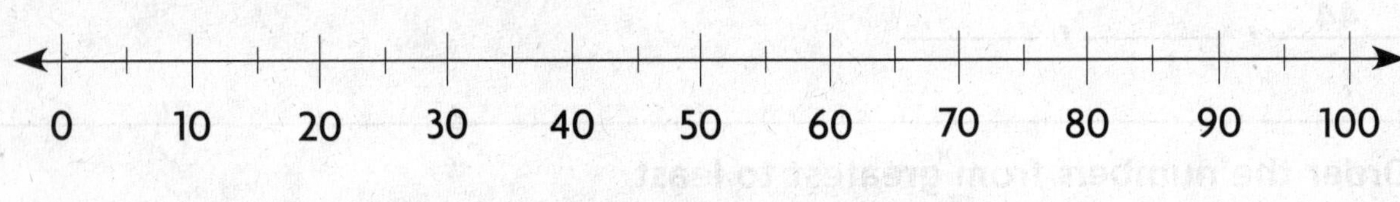

_____, _____, _____

4. 69 21 92 76

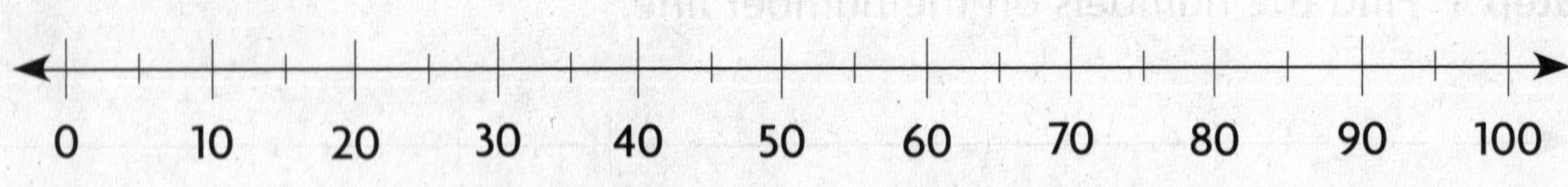

_____, _____, _____, _____

Check

5. Look back at Problem 4. Which number is the least? Which number is the greatest? How do you know?

____

____

____

Name_______________________________

Addition Facts and Strategies

Skill 5

Learn the Math

You can use different strategies to find the sum of two numbers.

$$\begin{array}{r} 3 \\ +\ 3 \\ \hline \end{array} \qquad \begin{array}{r} 3 \\ +\ 4 \\ \hline \end{array} \qquad \begin{array}{r} 7 \\ +\ 5 \\ \hline \end{array}$$

Vocabulary

- addend
- doubles
- doubles plus one
- make a ten

Doubles

Find 3 + 3.

The addends are the same in a doubles fact.

3 + 3 = 6

Doubles Plus One

Find 3 + 4.

One of the addends is 1 more in a double-plus-one fact.

3 + 4 = 7

or

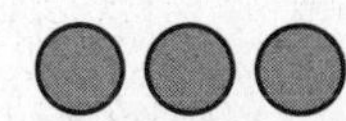

4 + 3 = 7

Make a Ten

Find 7 + 5.

Use a ten frame.
Put in 7 counters.
Put 5 counters below.

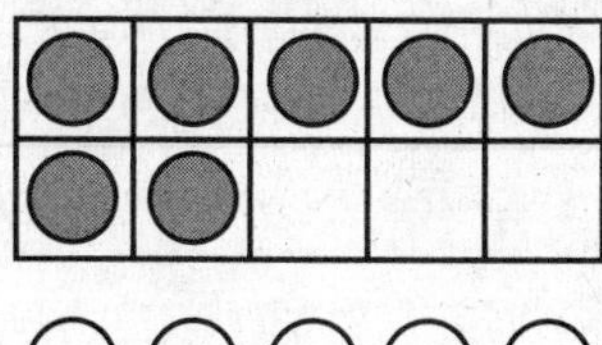

Then make a ten.
Move 3 counters to fill the ten frame.

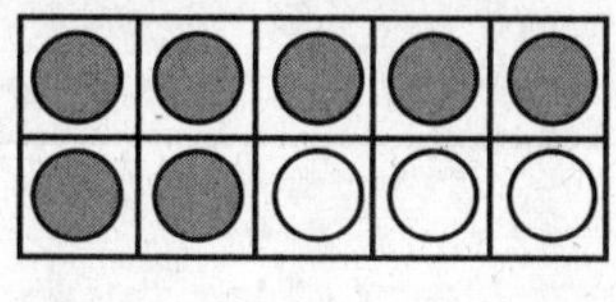

Now you have 10 and 2.
10 + 2 = 12
So, 7 + 5 = ______.

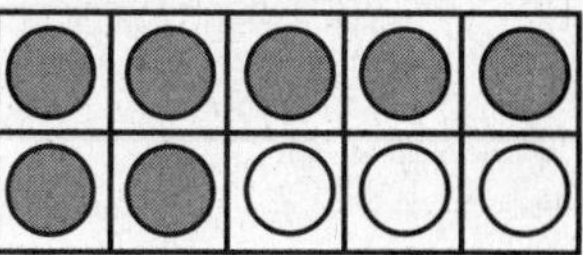

Find the sum. Use doubles, doubles plus one, or make a ten.

1. $5 + 5$

2. $5 + 6$

3. $9 + 3$

4. $6 + 7$

5. $9 + 6$

6. $8 + 8$

7. $9 + 8$

8. $8 + 9$

9. $6 + 6$

10. $7 + 6$

11. $8 + 5$

12. $7 + 5$

13. $3 + 3$

14. $2 + 3$

15. $6 + 7$

16. $8 + 4$

Check

17. How did you find the sum in Problem 4? Use a drawing to explain.

____

____

Name ____________________

Practice Addition Facts

Skill 6

Vocabulary

addend

Learn the Math

You can use patterns and rules to find sums.

Any number plus zero equals that number.

1 + 0 = 1　　5 + 0 = _____

2 + 0 = 2　　6 + 0 = _____

3 + 0 = 3　　7 + 0 = _____

4 + 0 = 4　　8 + 0 = _____

Changing the order of the addends does not change the sum.

7 + 8 = 15　　3 + 9 = _____

8 + 7 = 15　　9 + 3 = 12

4 + 5 = 9　　8 + 6 = 14

5 + 4 = _____　　6 + 8 = _____

Adding 1 to one of the addends in a double increases the sum by one.

6 + 6 = 12　　4 + 4 = 8

6 + 7 = 13　　4 + 5 = _____

8 + 8 = 16　　9 + 9 = 18

8 + 9 = _____　　9 + 10 = _____

Do the Math

Find the sums.

1. 3 + 3 = ____
   3 + 4 = ____

2. 9 + 0 = ____
   0 + 9 = ____

3. 9 + 5 = ____
   5 + 9 = ____

4. 5 + 5 = ____
   5 + 6 = ____

5. 0 + 5 = ____
   5 + 0 = ____

6. 8 + 9 = ____
   9 + 8 = ____

7. 6 + 6 = ____
   6 + 7 = ____

8. 3 + 5 = ____
   5 + 3 = ____

9. 3 + 9 = ____
   9 + 3 = ____

10. 8 + 0 = ____
    0 + 8 = ____

11. 4 + 5 = ____
    5 + 4 = ____

12. 2 + 2 = ____
    2 + 3 = ____

13. 3 + 5 = ____
    5 + 3 = ____

14. 7 + 7 = ____
    7 + 8 = ____

15. 0 + 7 = ____
    7 + 0 = ____

Check

16. What rule or pattern did you use to help you find the sums in Problem 3?

____

____

____

Name ____________________

Practice Subtraction Facts
Skill 7

Learn the Math

You can use addition and number lines to help you subtract.

Find the difference. 12 – 3

Use addition.

Use the related addition fact from the same fact family.

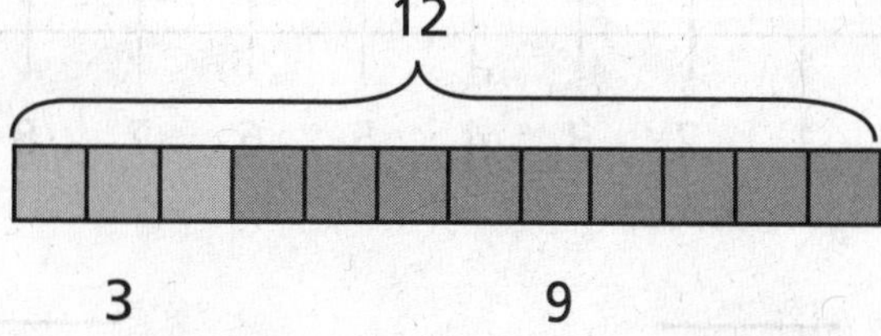

Think: 3 + 9 = 12

So, 12 – 3 = ______.

Use a number line.

Count back on a number line.

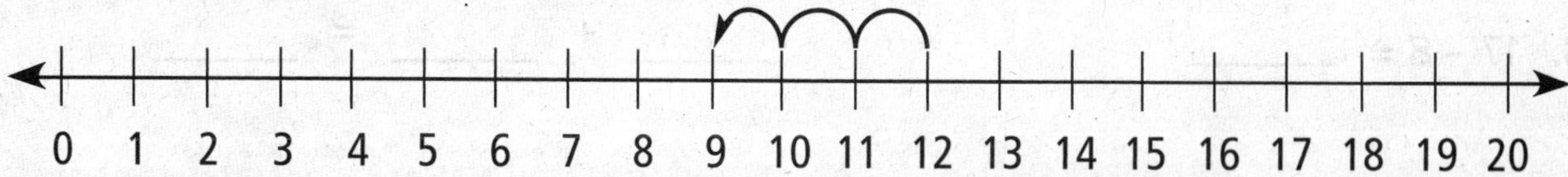

So, 12 – 3 = ______.

Find the difference. Use the number line. Then write a related addition fact.

11 – 2 = ▪

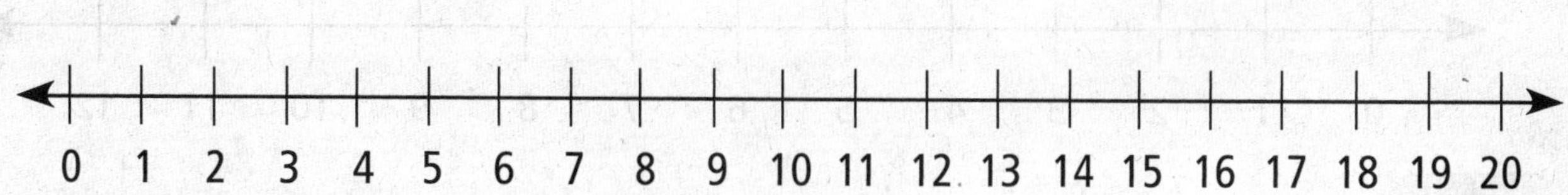

______ + ______ = ______

So, 11 – 2 = ______.

Find the difference. Use the number line.
Then write a related addition fact.

1. 15 – 9 = ______ ______ + ______ = ______

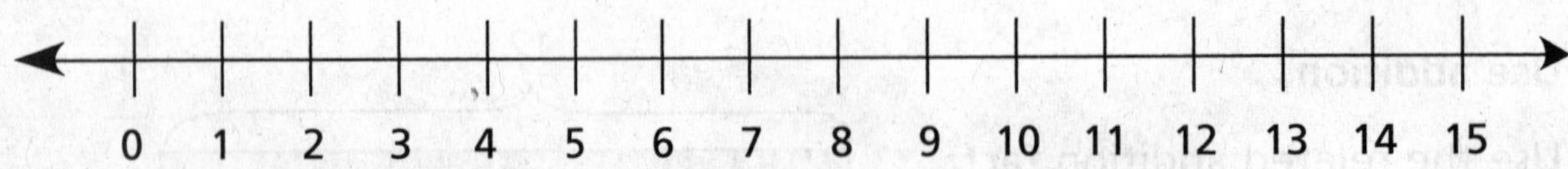

2. 10 – 2 = ______ ______ + ______ = ______

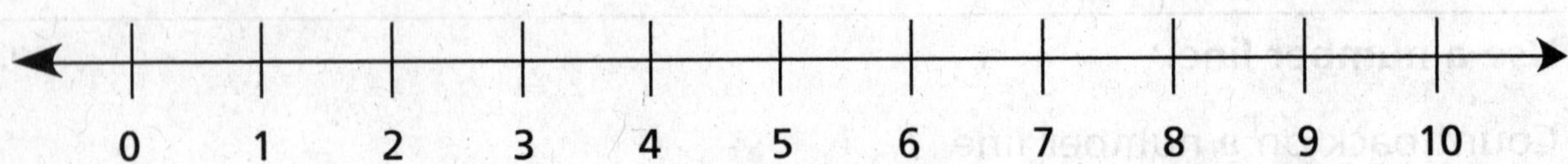

3. 17 – 8 = ______ ______ + ______ = ______

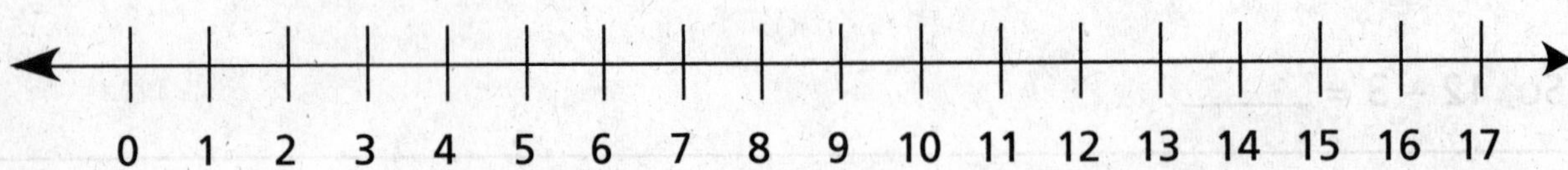

4. 12 – 7 = ______ ______ + ______ = ______

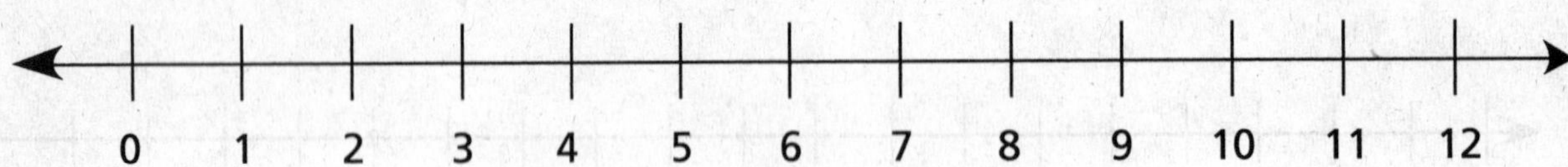

Check

5. Look at Problem 4. Explain how you got your answer.

______

______

______

Name ______________________________

Model 2-Digit Addition

Skill 8

Learn the Math

Find 25 + 34.

Use base-ten blocks.

Step 1 Show 25 and 34.
Add the ones.

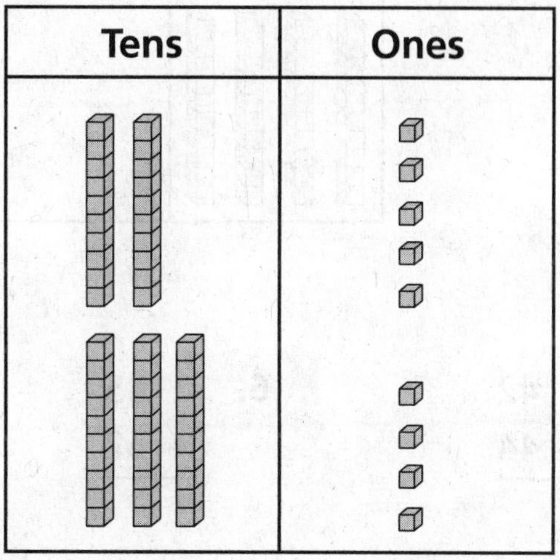

Tens	Ones
2 tens	5 ones
3 tens	4 ones

5 ones + 4 ones = ______ ones

	Tens	Ones
	2	5
+	3	4
		9

Step 2 Add the tens.

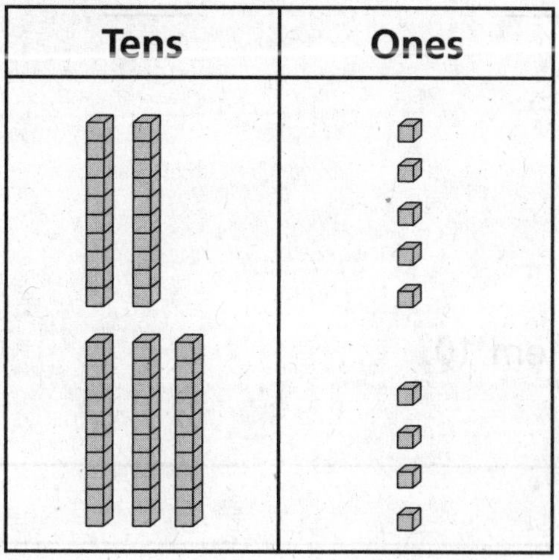

Tens	Ones
2 tens	5 ones
3 tens	4 ones

2 tens + 3 tens = ______ tens

	Tens	Ones
	2	5
+	3	4
	5	9

So, 25 + 34 = ______.

Do the Math

Use base-ten blocks to find the sum.

1. 13
+ 25

Tens	Ones

2. 39
+ 40

Tens	Ones

Find the sum.

3. 12
+ 14

4. 13
+ 42

5. 42
+ 44

6. 35
+ 52

7. 47
+ 31

8. 54
+ 34

9. 65
+ 24

10. 73
+ 26

Check

11. Explain how you got your answer for Problem 10.

____

____

____

Name ______________________________

2-Digit Addition With Regrouping

Skill 9

Vocabulary

regroup

Learn the Math

Find 35 + 26.
Use base-ten blocks.

Step 1 Show 35 and 26. Add the ones.

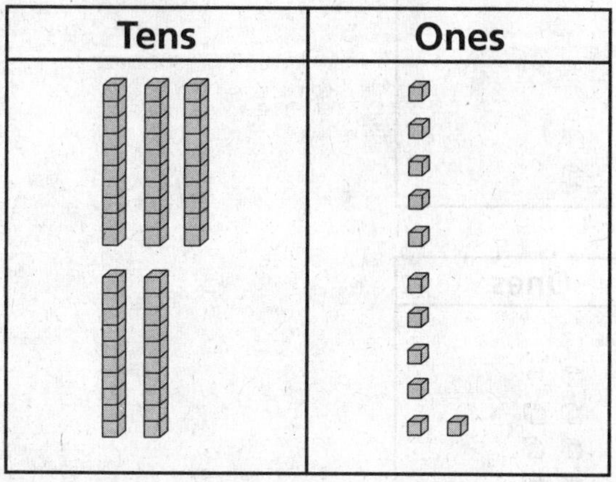

Tens	Ones
3 tens, 2 tens	5 ones, 6 ones

5 + 6 = _____

	Tens	Ones
	☐	
	3	5
+	2	6

Step 2 Regroup.

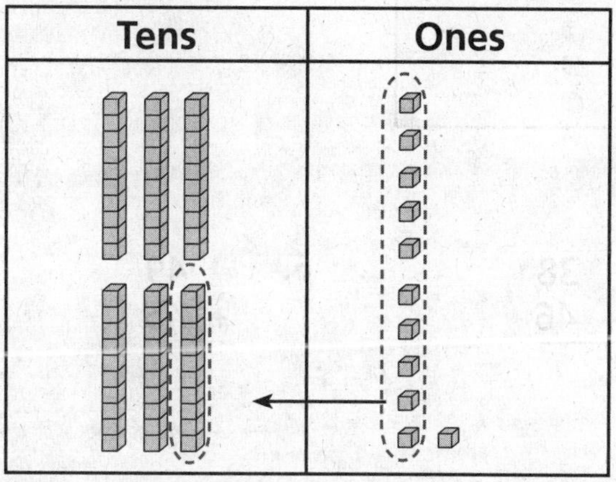

Tens	Ones

11 ones = 1 ten 1 one

	Tens	Ones
	1	
	3	5
+	2	6
		1

Step 3 Add the tens.

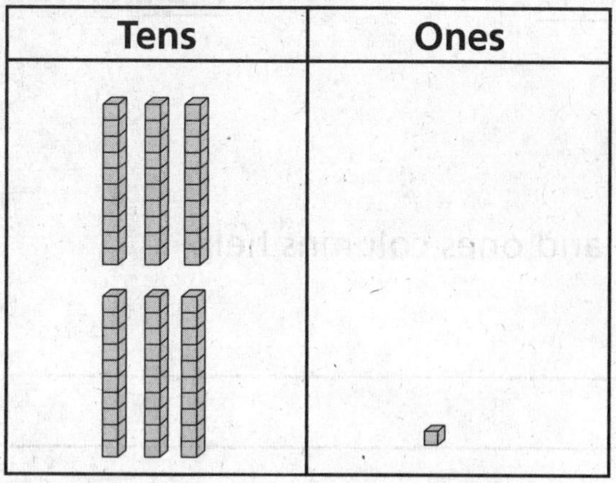

Tens	Ones

1 + 3 + 2 = _____

	Tens	Ones
	1	
	3	5
+	2	6
	6	1

So, 35 + 26 = _______ .

Use base-ten blocks to find the sum.

1. $\begin{array}{r} 19 \\ +\ 62 \\ \hline \end{array}$

Tens	Ones

2. $\begin{array}{r} 68 \\ +\ 24 \\ \hline \end{array}$

Tens	Ones

Find the sum.

3. $\begin{array}{r} 46 \\ +\ 24 \\ \hline \end{array}$

4. $\begin{array}{r} 49 \\ +\ 34 \\ \hline \end{array}$

5. $\begin{array}{r} 38 \\ +\ 46 \\ \hline \end{array}$

6. $\begin{array}{r} 49 \\ +\ 45 \\ \hline \end{array}$

7. $\begin{array}{r} 18 \\ +\ 34 \\ \hline \end{array}$

8. $\begin{array}{r} 29 \\ +\ 36 \\ \hline \end{array}$

9. $\begin{array}{r} 73 \\ +\ 17 \\ \hline \end{array}$

10. $\begin{array}{r} 27 \\ +\ 34 \\ \hline \end{array}$

Check

11. How does lining up the digits in the tens and ones columns help when regrouping?

____

____

Name________________________________

Model 2-Digit Subtraction
Skill 10

Learn the Math

Find 48 – 26.
Use base-ten blocks.

Step 1 Show 48.

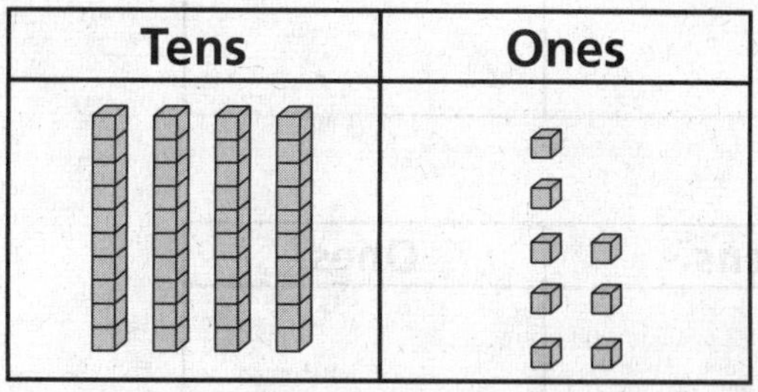

Tens	Ones

Step 2 Subtract the ones.

8 ones – 6 ones = ____ ones

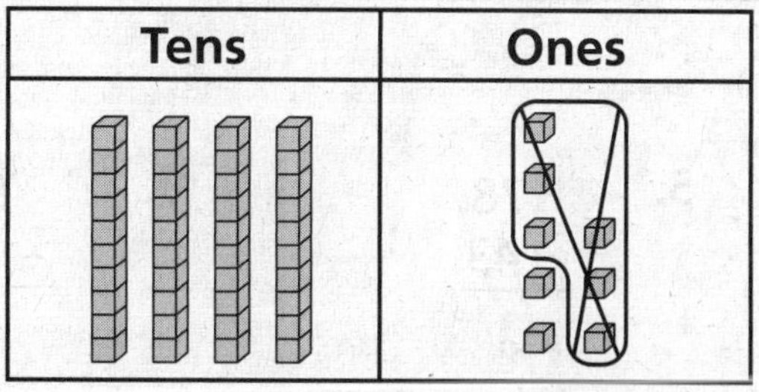

Tens	Ones

	Tens	Ones
	4	8
–	2	6
		2

Step 3 Subtract the tens.

4 tens – 2 tens = ____ tens

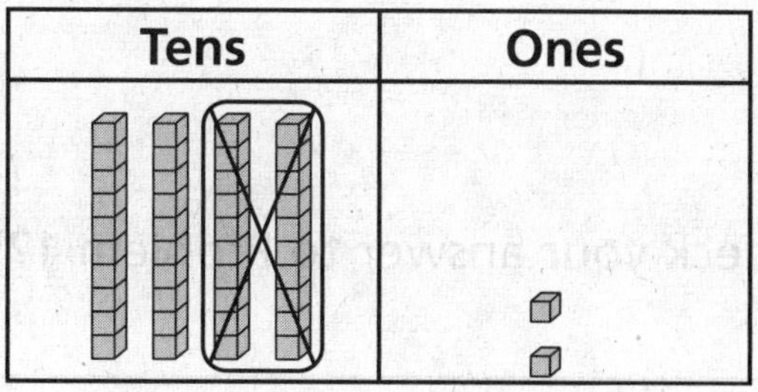

Tens	Ones

	Tens	Ones
	4	8
–	2	6
	2	2

So, 48 – 26 = ______.

Use base-ten blocks to find the difference.

1.
$$\begin{array}{r} 56 \\ -\ 13 \\ \hline \end{array}$$

Tens	Ones

2.
$$\begin{array}{r} 34 \\ -\ 21 \\ \hline \end{array}$$

Tens	Ones

Find the difference.

3. $\begin{array}{r} 67 \\ -\ 42 \\ \hline \end{array}$ **4.** $\begin{array}{r} 49 \\ -\ 36 \\ \hline \end{array}$ **5.** $\begin{array}{r} 78 \\ -\ 43 \\ \hline \end{array}$ **6.** $\begin{array}{r} 89 \\ -\ 39 \\ \hline \end{array}$

7. $\begin{array}{r} 89 \\ -\ 29 \\ \hline \end{array}$ **8.** $\begin{array}{r} 43 \\ -\ 11 \\ \hline \end{array}$ **9.** $\begin{array}{r} 65 \\ -\ 24 \\ \hline \end{array}$ **10.** $\begin{array}{r} 88 \\ -\ 32 \\ \hline \end{array}$

Check

11. How could you use addition to check your answer to Problem 1?

____

____

____

Name________________________________

Subtract 1-Digit from 2-Digit Numbers
Skill 11

Learn the Math

Find 26 – 8.
Use base-ten blocks.

Step 1

Show 26.

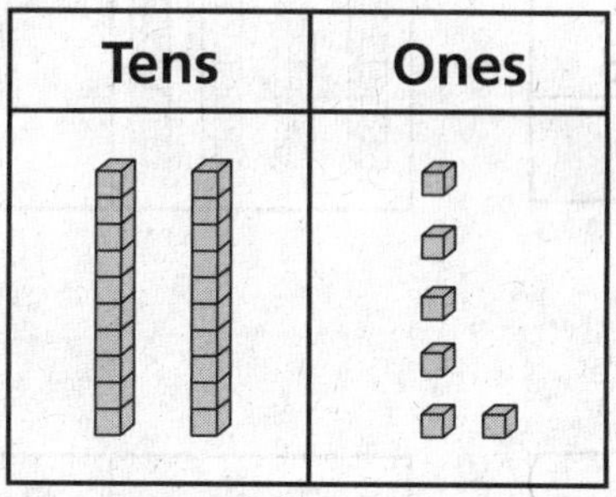

Tens	Ones
2	6
–	8

Step 2

8 ones > 6 ones, so regroup 1 ten as 10 ones.

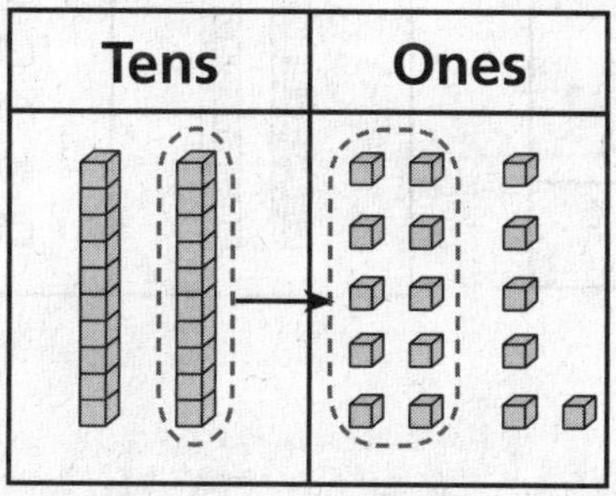

Tens	Ones
1	16
~~2~~	~~6~~
–	8

Step 3

Subtract the ones.

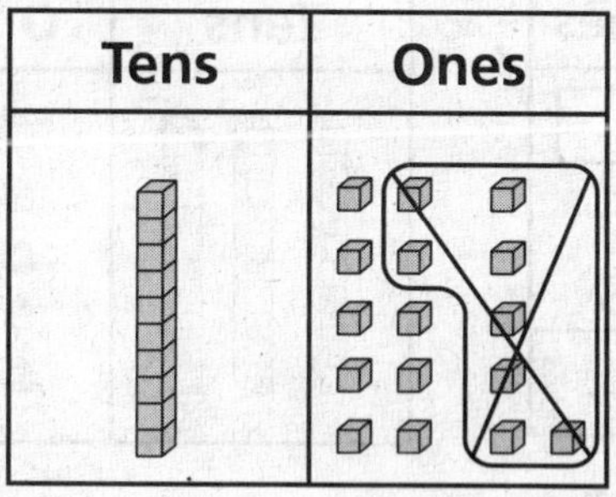

Tens	Ones
1	16
~~2~~	~~6~~
–	8
	8

Step 4

Subtract the tens.

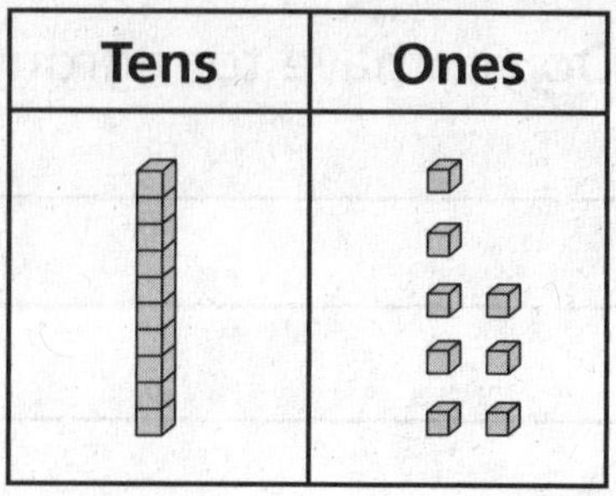

Tens	Ones
1	16
~~2~~	~~6~~
–	8
1	8

So, 26 – 8 = _____.

Use base-ten blocks to find the difference.

1.

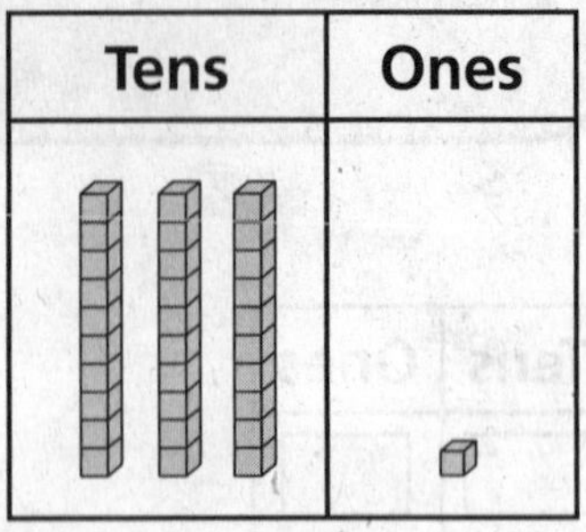

Tens	Ones
☐	☐
3	1
−	8

2.

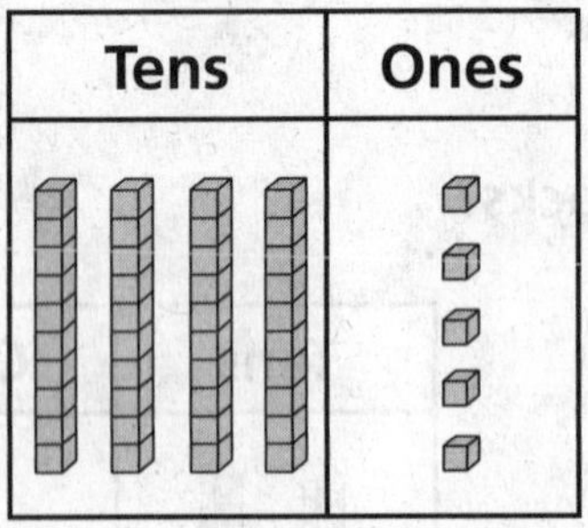

Tens	Ones
☐	☐
4	5
−	9

3.

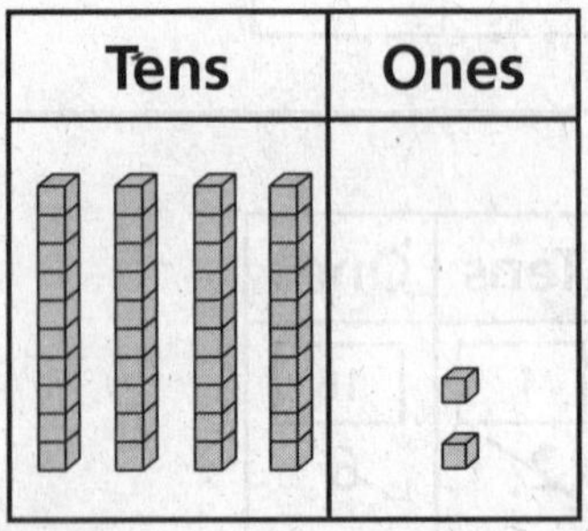

Tens	Ones
☐	☐
4	2
−	9

4.

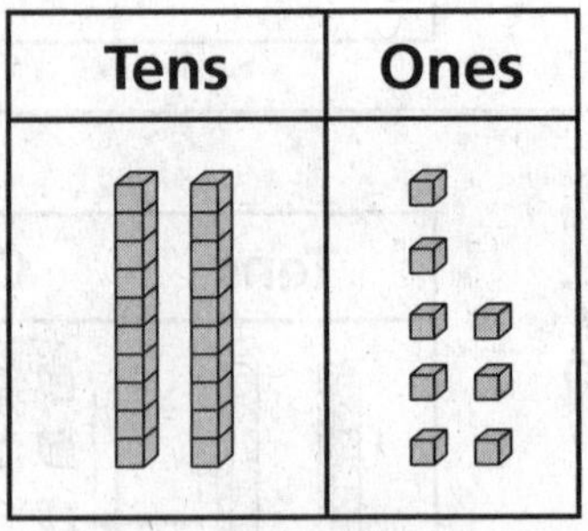

Tens	Ones
☐	☐
2	8
−	9

5.

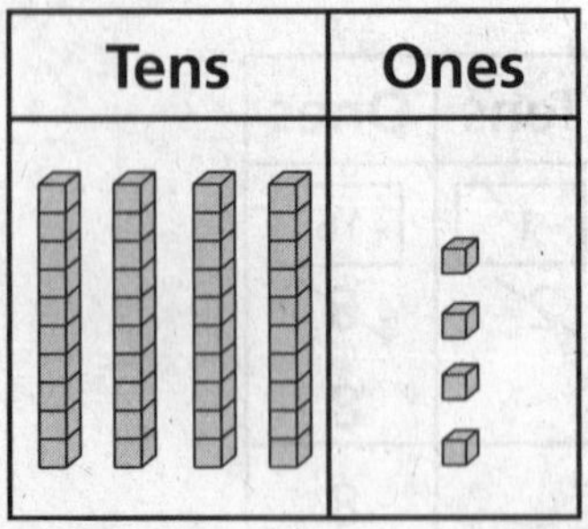

Tens	Ones
☐	☐
4	4
−	8

6.

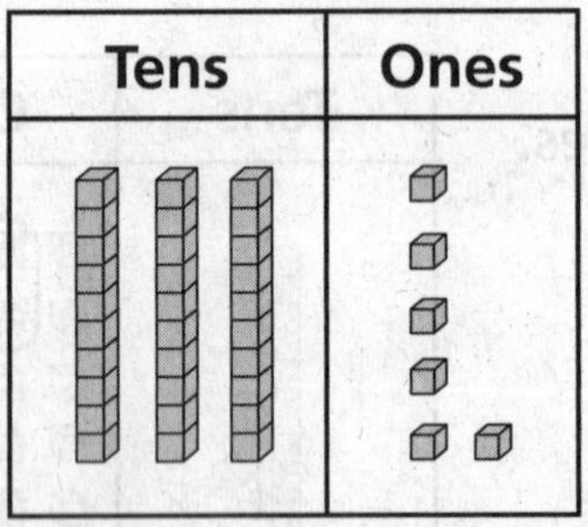

Tens	Ones
☐	☐
3	6
−	7

Check

7. You want to subtract 7 from 39. Do you have to regroup? Explain.

____

____

____

Name______________________________________

Learn the Math

Find 35 – 16.
Use base-ten blocks.

Vocabulary

regroup

Step 1

Show 35. Are there enough ones to subtract 6?

	Tens	Ones
	☐	☐
	3	5
–	1	6

Step 2

If there are not enough ones, regroup 1 ten as 10 ones.

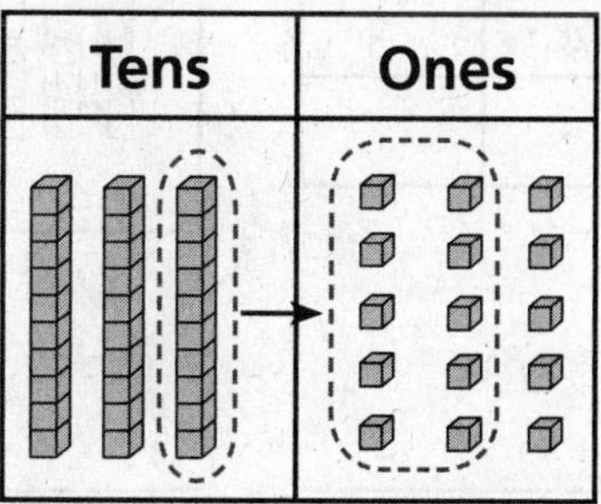

	Tens	Ones
	2	15
	~~3~~	~~5~~
–	1	6

Step 3

Subtract the ones.

	Tens	Ones
	2	15
	~~3~~	~~5~~
–	1	6
		9

Step 4

Subtract the tens.

	Tens	Ones
	2	15
	~~3~~	~~5~~
–	1	6
	1	9

So, 35 – 16 = ______ .

Do the Math

Use base-ten blocks to find the difference.

1.

Tens	Ones
4	1
− 2	5

2.

Tens	Ones
6	7
− 4	2

3.

Tens	Ones
5	2
− 4	3

4.

Tens	Ones
4	4
− 3	6

5.

Tens	Ones
5	8
− 2	6

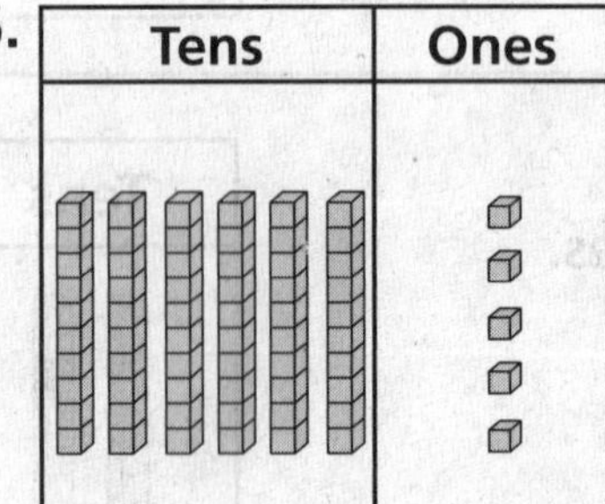

6.

Tens	Ones
6	5
− 3	2

Check

7. Do you always need to regroup when you subtract? Explain. Give an example.

Name ________________________________

Skip-Count

Skill 13

Learn the Math

You can use a number line to skip-count.

Vocabulary

Skip-count by twos. Start at 35.

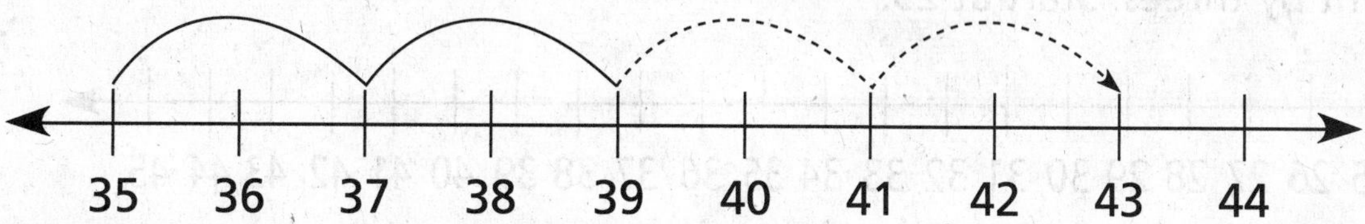

35, 37, 39, <u>41</u>, <u>43</u>

Skip-count by threes. Start at 21.

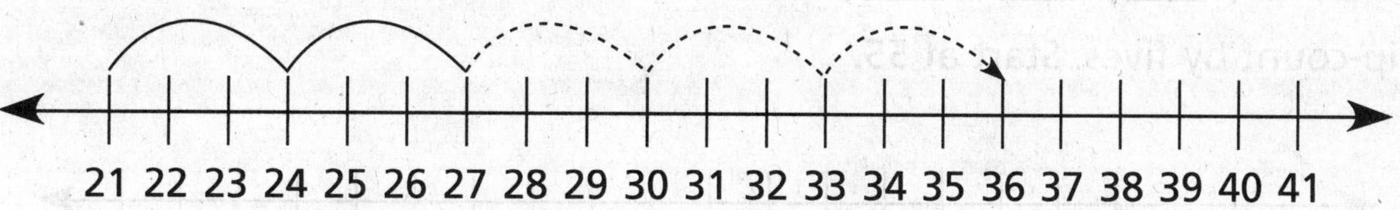

21, 24, 27, ____, ____, ____

Skip-count by fives. Start at 43. Write the missing numbers.

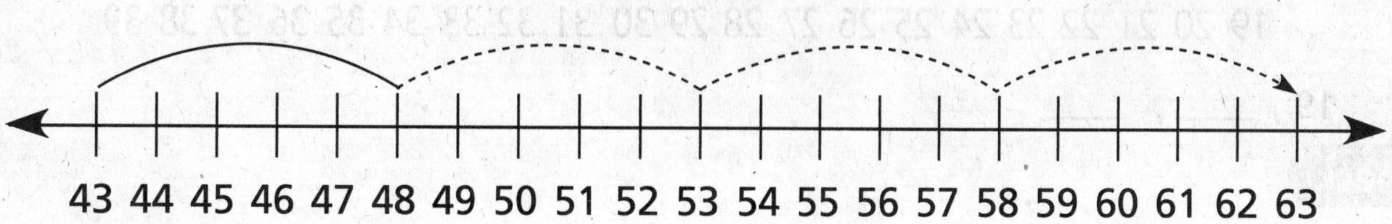

43, 48, ____, 58, ____

Do the Math

Use the number line to skip-count. Find the missing numbers.

1. Skip-count by twos. Start at 17.

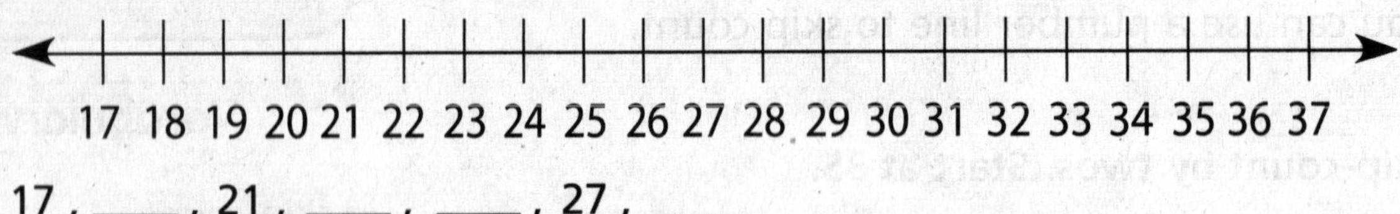

17, ____, 21, ____, ____, 27, ____

2. Skip-count by threes. Start at 25.

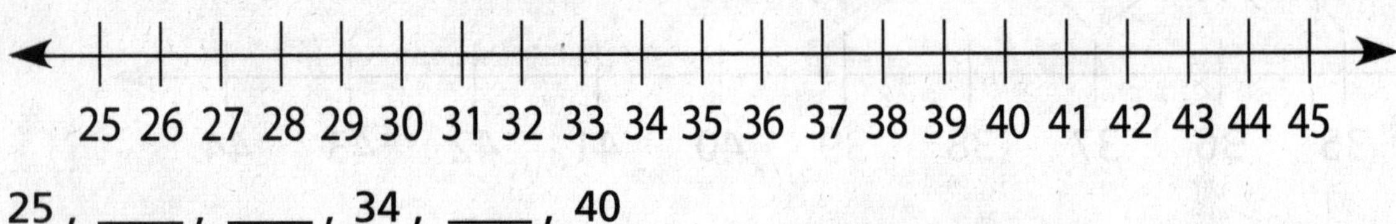

25, ____, ____, 34, ____, 40

3. Skip-count by fours. Start at 12.

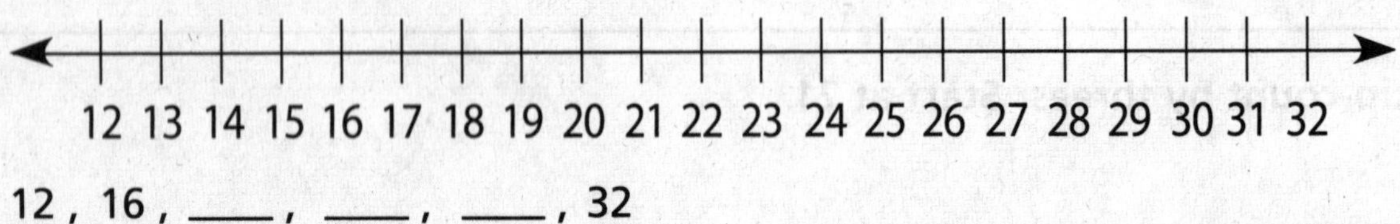

12, 16, ____, ____, ____, 32

4. Skip-count by fives. Start at 55.

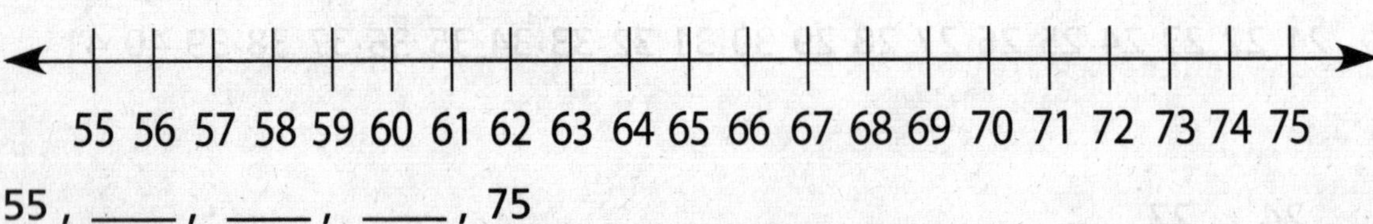

55, ____, ____, ____, 75

5. Skip-count by tens. Start at 19.

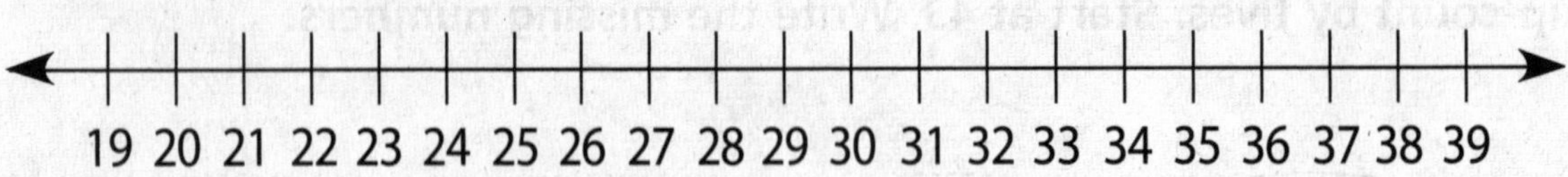

19, ____, ____

Check

6. Look at Problem 2. Jenny started at 25, but the first number she wrote was 29. What mistake did Jenny make?

____

____

Name________________________________

Find a Number Pattern

Skill 14

Learn the Math

Vocabulary

pattern

A pattern is an ordered set of numbers or objects.
A rule can be used to describe a pattern.

Find the missing number. 30, 60, 90, 120, 

Step 1 Look at the number pattern. What is the rule?

Think: How does each number relate to the next number in the pattern?

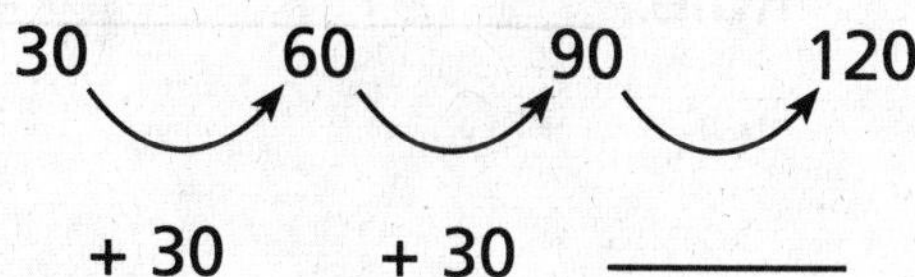

+ 30 + 30 ______

The numbers increase by thirty.

So, the rule is *add* ______.

Step 2 Use the rule to extend the pattern.

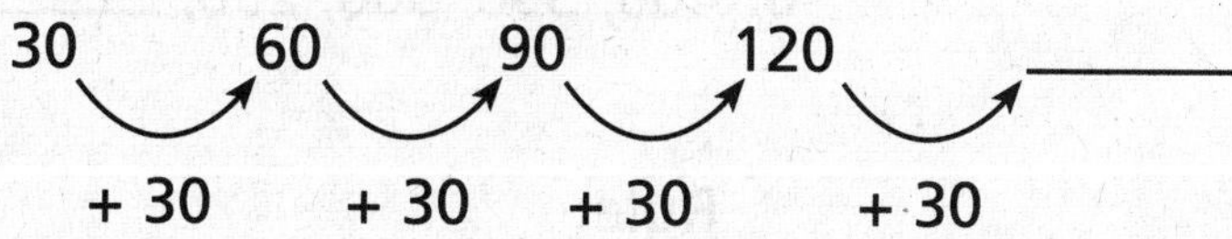

+ 30 + 30 + 30 + 30

So, the missing number is 120 + 30, or ______.

Find the missing number. 75, 60, 45, 30, ■

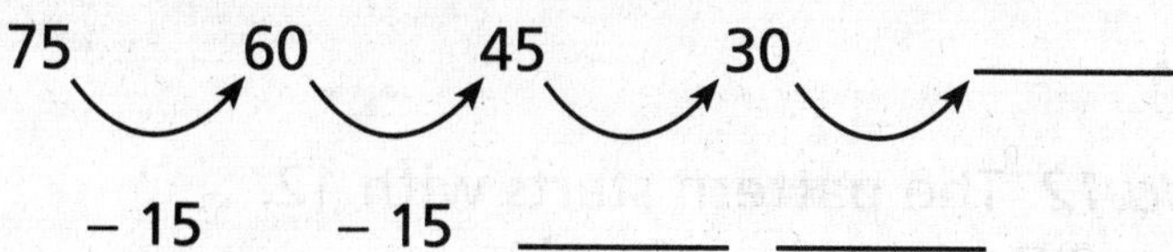

– 15 – 15 ______ ______

Rule: ________________

Missing number: ______

Do the Math

Find the missing number in each pattern. Write the rule.

1. 3, 6, 9, 12, ______

Rule: ____________________

2. 100, 85, 70, 55, ______

Rule: ____________________

3. 20, 40, 60, 80, ______

Rule: ____________________

4. 20, 15, 10, 5, ______

Rule: ____________________

5. 15, 25, 35, 45, ______

Rule: ____________________

6. 25, 50, 75, 100, ______

Rule: ____________________

7. 300, 400, 500, 600, ______

Rule: ____________________

8. 400, 350, 300, 250, ______

Rule: ____________________

9. 200, 202, 204, 206, ______

Rule: ____________________

10. 40, 32, 24, 16, ______

Rule: ____________________

Check

11. The rule for a pattern is *add 12*. The pattern starts with 12. What are the next 3 numbers? Explain.

____

____

____

Name_______________________________________

Equal Groups
Skill 15

Learn the Math

Find how many in all.
2 groups of 6

Step 1 Use counters to model.
Think: Make 2 groups with 6 counters in each group.

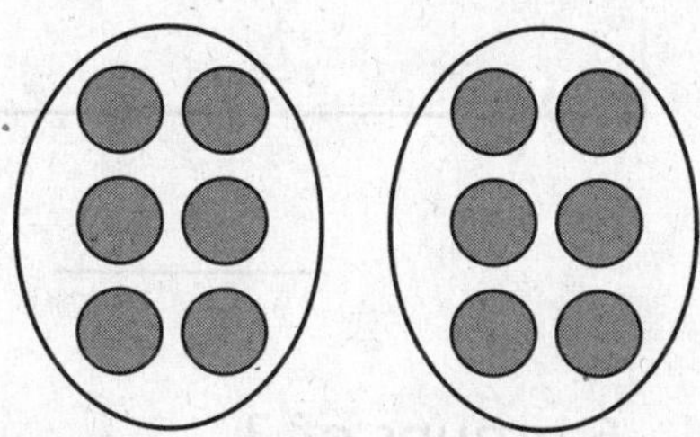

Step 2 Count the total number of counters.

There are ______ counters in all.

Vocabulary

equal groups

Find how many in all.
3 groups of 5

Step 1 Use stars to model.
Think: Make 3 groups with 5 stars in each group.

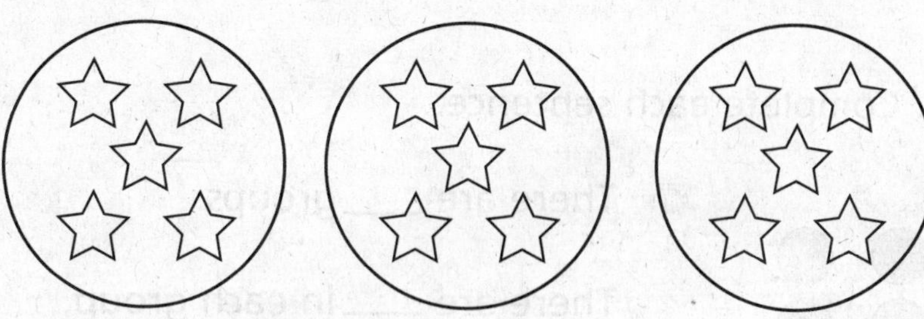

Step 2 Count the total number of stars.

There are ______ stars in all.

Do the Math

Find how many in all. You may wish to draw a picture.

1. 9 groups of 2

____

2. 3 groups of 4

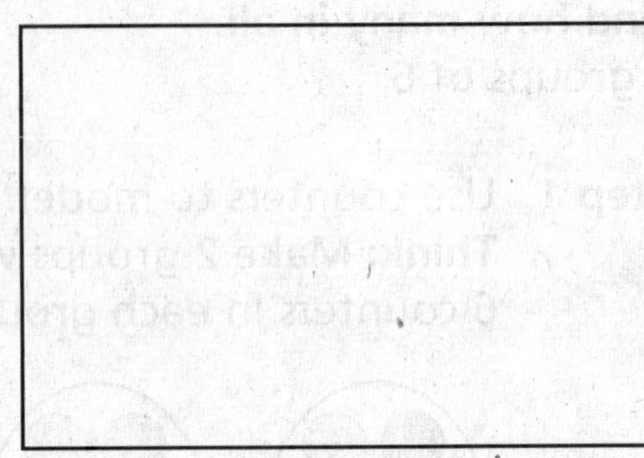

____

3. 2 groups of 5

____

4. 6 groups of 3

____

Check

5. Circle equal groups. Complete each sentence.

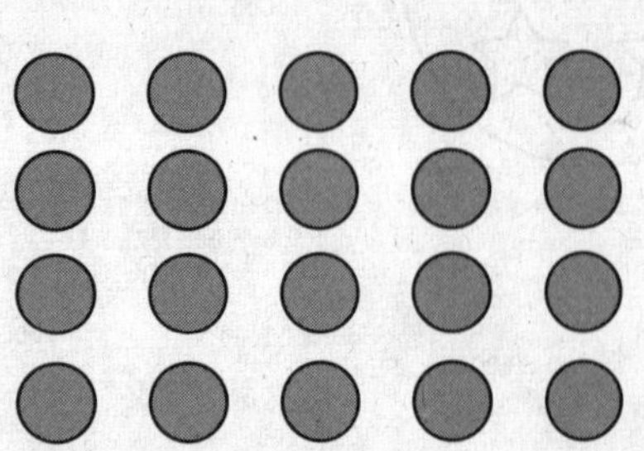

There are ____ groups.

There are ____ in each group.

There are ____ counters.

Name ____________________

Relate Addition to Multiplication

Skill 16

Learn the Math

You can add or multiply to find the total number of items in equal groups.

Vocabulary

equal groups
multiply
product
sum

There are 4 bananas in a bunch. There are 3 bunches of bananas. How many bananas are there in all?

You can use addition or multiplication to find how many bananas there are in all.

Use counters to show equal groups.

3 groups of 4 counters

Use repeated addition to find the sum. $4 + 4 + 4 =$ ____

Or, write a multiplication sentence to find the product. $3 \times 4 =$ ____

$4 + 4 + 4 =$ ____ and $3 \times 4 =$ ____

So, there are ____ bananas in all.

Do the Math

Draw equal groups. Find the sum. Then find the product.

1. 2 groups of 5

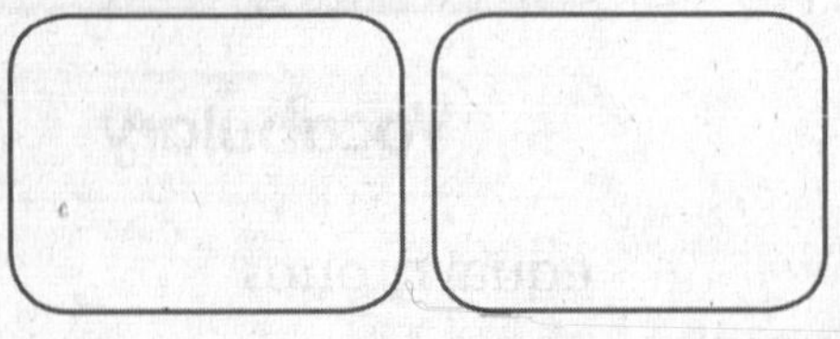

5 + 5 = ____

2 × 5 = ____

2. 3 groups of 3

3 + 3 + 3 = ____

3 × 3 = ____

3. 4 groups of 2

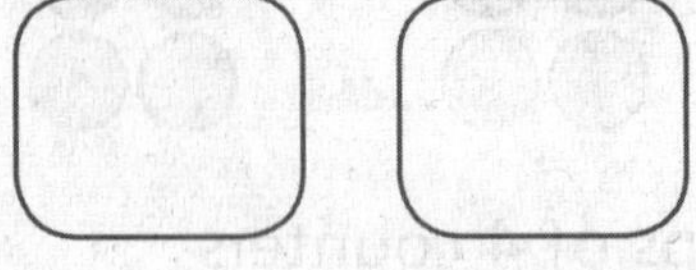

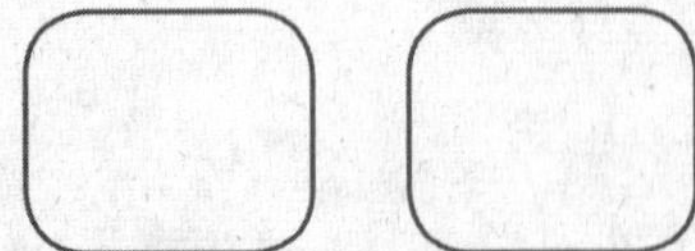

2 + 2 + 2 + 2 = ____

4 × 2 = ____

4. 5 groups of 1

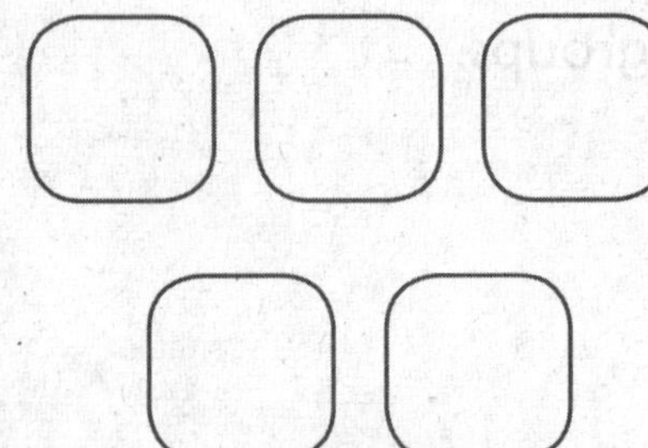

1 + 1 + 1 + 1 + 1 = ____

5 × 1 = ____

Check

5. Can you multiply to find how many stars there are in all? Explain.

____

____

____

Name________________________________

Arrays

Skill 17

Learn the Math

You can use an array to multiply.

Vocabulary

array
Commutative Property of Multiplication
factor
product

Use an array to multiply. 3 × 6

Use tiles. Make 3 rows with 6 tiles in each row.

Count the number of tiles.

How many tiles are there in all? ____

$3 \times 6 =$ ____

column

row

3 rows of 6

You can turn the array to show 6 rows of 3.

Count the number of tiles.

$6 \times 3 =$ ____

6 rows of 3

The Commutative Property of Multiplication, or Order Property of Multiplication, states that factors can be multiplied in any order and their product is the same.

$3 \times 6 = 18$ and $6 \times 3 = 18$

Do the Math

Write a multiplication sentence for each array.

1.

2.

Write the multiplication sentence for the array.
Then draw the array that shows the Commutative Property.

3.

4.

Check

5. On another sheet of paper, draw an array that has 7 rows with 2 in each row. Then draw an array that has 2 rows with 7 in each row. Write the multiplication sentences. How are they the same? How are they different?

Name________________________________

Multiply with 2 and 4

Skill 18

Learn the Math

You can use a number line to multiply.

Find 2 × 4.

Start at 0. Make 2 jumps of 4 spaces each on the number line.

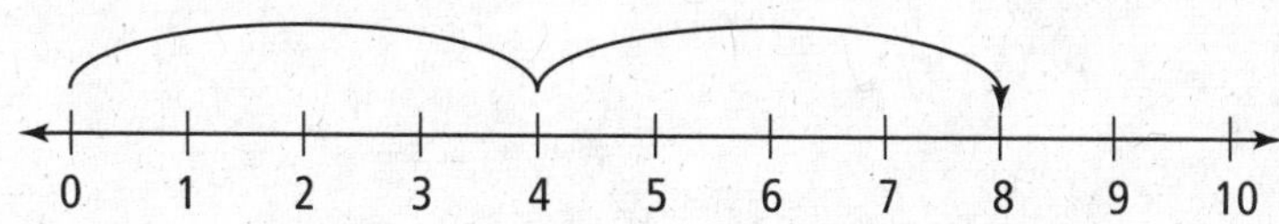

The last number you landed on is the product.

What is the last number you landed on? ____

So, 2 × 4 = ____ .

Use the number line.
Find 4 × 2.

Start at 0. Make 4 jumps of 2 spaces each on the number line.

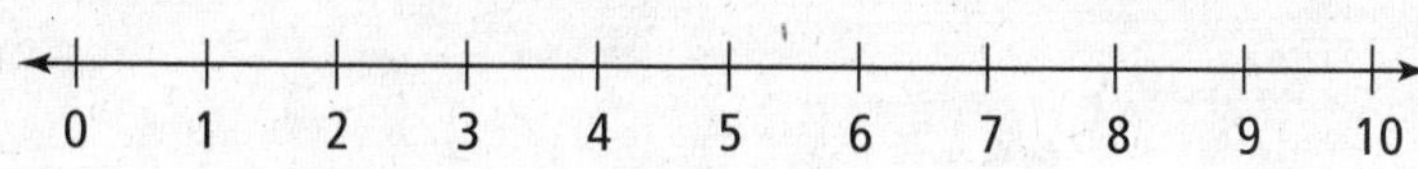

So, 4 × 2 = ____ .

Do the Math

Use the number line to find the product.

1. 2 × 7 = ____

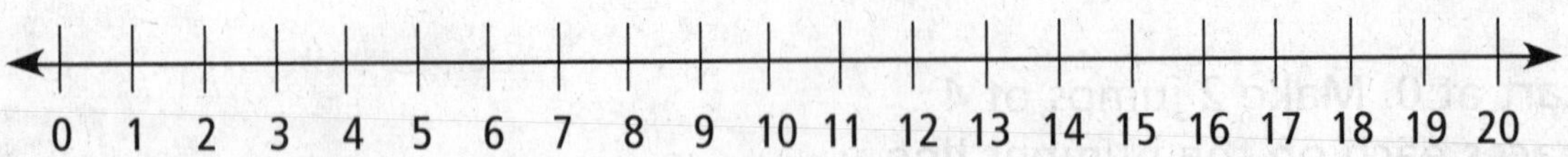

2. 4 × 5 = ____

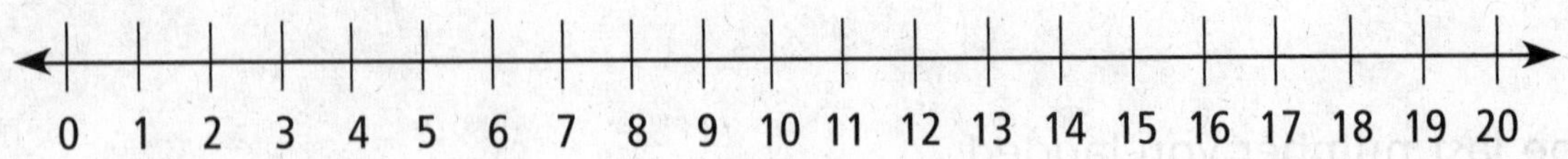

3. 4 × 3 = ____

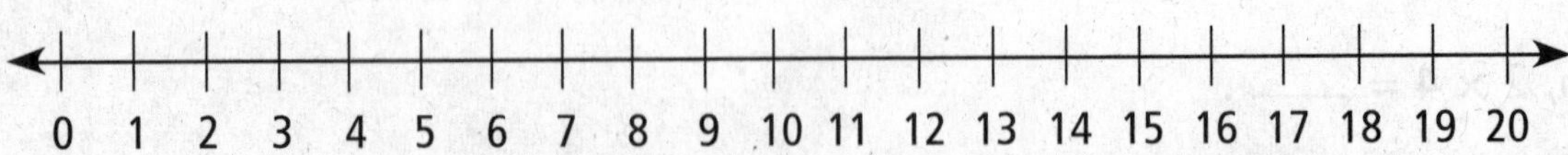

4. 9 × 2 = ____

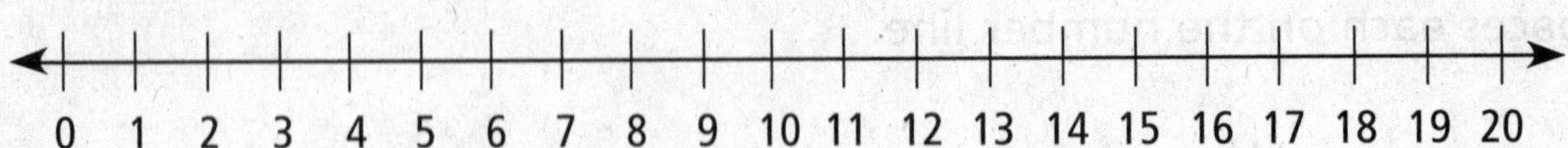

Check

5. Look at your answer for Problem 4. Show another way you can make equal jumps to land on the same product.

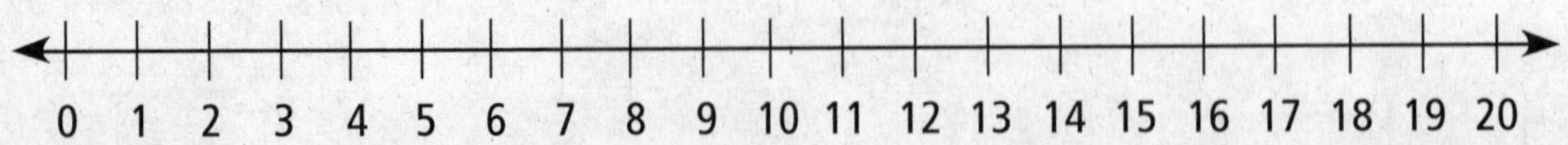

Name____

Learn the Math

There are many ways to find a product.

Find 2 × 6.

Use counters.

Make 2 rows of 6 counters.

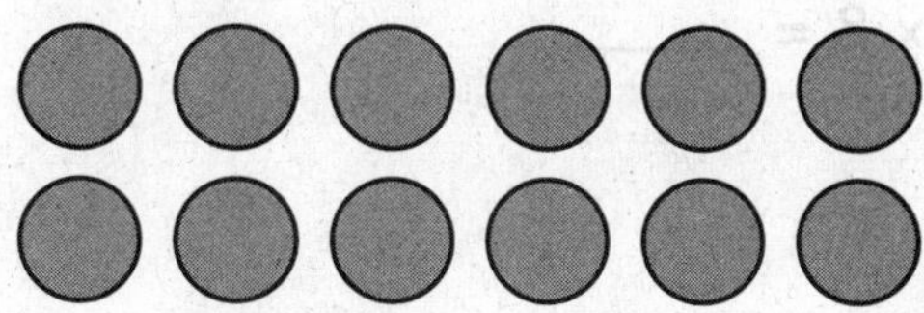

Think: 2 rows of 6

6 + 6

Write: 2 × 6 = **12**

$$\begin{array}{r} 6 \\ \times\ 2 \\ \hline \mathbf{12} \end{array}$$

Draw a picture.

Draw 2 groups of 6.

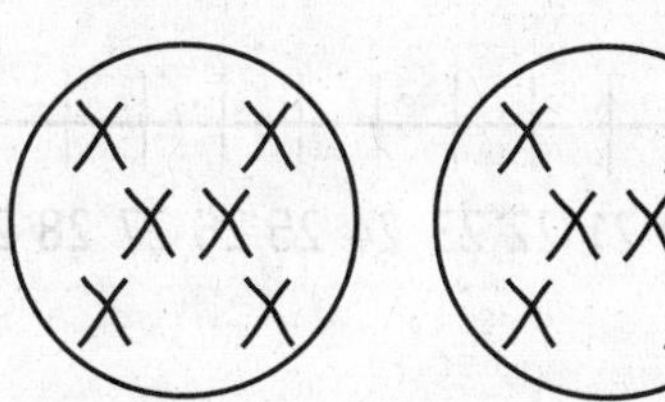

Think: 2 groups of 6

6 + 6

Write: 2 × 6 = _____

$$\begin{array}{r} 6 \\ \times\ 2 \\ \hline \end{array}$$

Use a number line.

Skip-count by sixes 2 times.

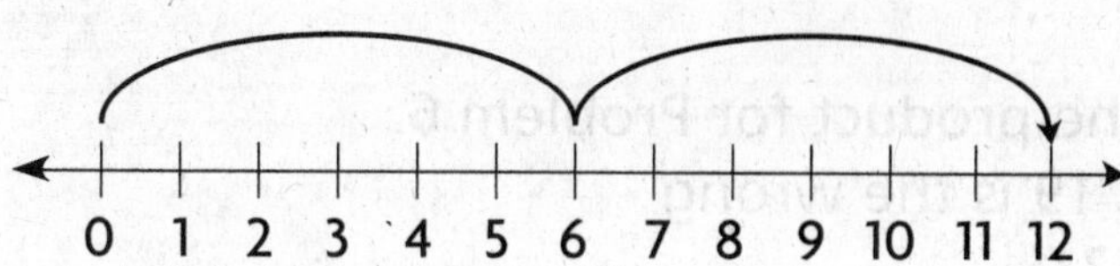

Think: Skip-count by 6.

6, 12

Write: 2 × 6 = _____

$$\begin{array}{r} 6 \\ \times\ 2 \\ \hline \end{array}$$

So, 2 × 6 = _____ .

Do the Math

Find the product. Use counters or draw a picture.

1. 2 × 5 = ______

2. 5 × 4 = ______

3. 2 × 8 = ______

4. 5 × 8 = ______

Find the product. Use the number line.

5. 5 × 5 = ______

6. 2 × 9 = ______

Check

7. Jennifer used a number line to find the product for Problem 6. She landed on 19. How do you know 19 is the wrong answer? What was Jennifer's mistake?

____

____

____

Name ______________________________

Multiply with 1 and 0

Skill 20

Learn the Math

The Identity Property of Multiplication states that the product of any number and 1 is that number. Such as 1 × 7 = 7 and 7 × 1 = 7.

Vocabulary

Identity Property of Multiplication

Zero Property of Multiplication

Use counters.
Find 5 × 1.

Step 1 Make a model.

Step 2 Write the multiplication sentence.
5 groups
1 counter in each group

____counters in all
5 × 1 = 5

So, 5 × 1 = ____.

The Zero Property of Multiplication states that the product of zero and any number is zero. Such as 5 × 0 = 0 and 0 × 5 = 0.

Write a multiplication sentence.
Find 6 × 0.

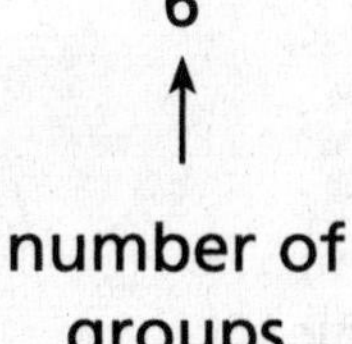
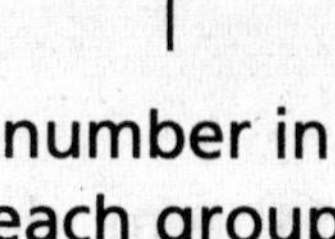
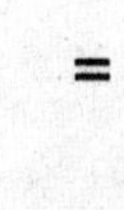
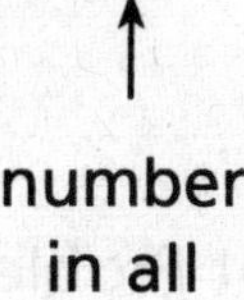

6 × 0 = 0

number of groups — number in each group — number in all

So, 6 × 0 = ____.

Find the product.

1. 0 × 5 = ____

2. 10 × 1 = ____

3. 1 × 9 = ____

4. 2 × 1 = ____

5. 0 × 3 = ____

6. 6 × 0 = ____

7. 4 × 1 = ____

8. 7 × 1 = ____

9. 1 × 0 = ____

10. 1 × 8 = ____

Check

11. Look at Problem 2. How would the model for 10 × 1 look different than the model for 1 × 10?

____

____

____

Name______________________________

Multiply with 4

Skill 21

Learn the Math

You can multiply with 4 in different ways.

Find 4 × 4.

Use counters.	**Think:**	**Write:**
Make 4 groups of 4 counters.	4 groups of 4 4 + 4 + 4 + 4	4 × 4 = 16 $\begin{array}{r} 4 \\ \times 4 \\ \hline 16 \end{array}$

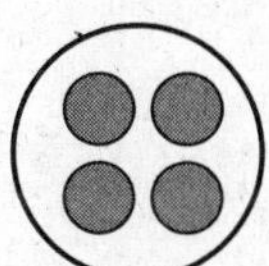 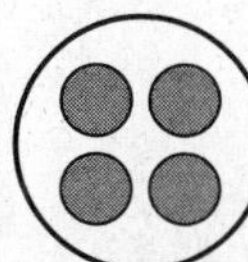 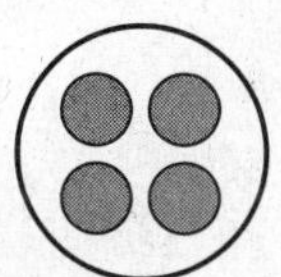 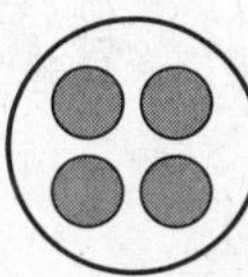

Draw a picture.	**Think:**	**Write:**
Draw 4 groups of 4.	4 groups of 4 4 + 4 + 4 + 4	4 × 4 = 16 $\begin{array}{r} 4 \\ \times 4 \\ \hline \end{array}$

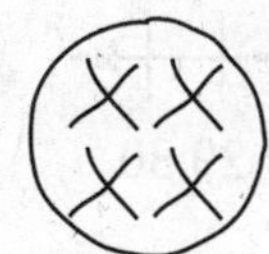  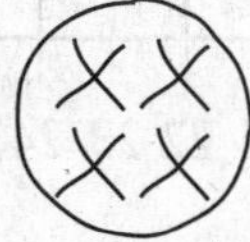 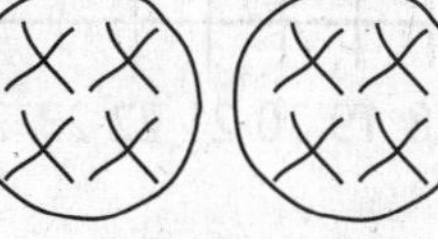

Use a number line.	**Think:**	**Write:**
Skip-count by four 4 times.	4, 8, 12, 16	4 × 4 = 16 $\begin{array}{r} 4 \\ \times 4 \\ \hline \end{array}$

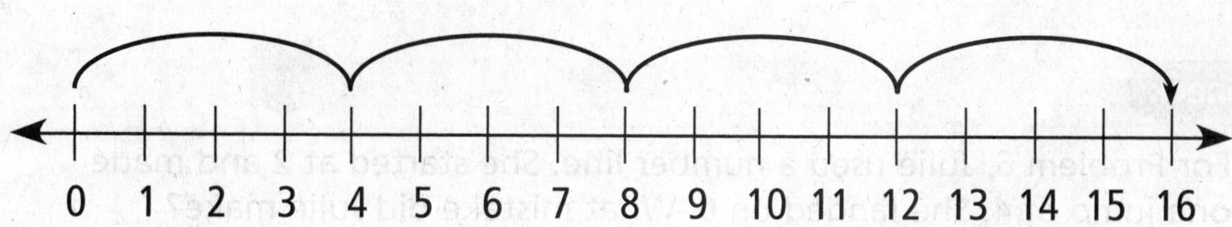

So, 4 × 4 = ____ .

Do the Math

Skill 21

Find the product. Use counters or draw a picture.

1. 4 × 3 = _____

2. 4 × 5 = _____

3. 4 × 7 = _____

4. 9 × 4 = _____

Find the product. Use the number line.

5. 4 × 6 = _____

6. 2 × 4 = _____

Check

7. For Problem 6, Julie used a number line. She started at 2 and made one jump of 4. She landed on 6. What mistake did Julie make?

____

____

____

Name ______________________________

Multiply with 6

Skill 22

Learn the Math

You can multiply with 6 in different ways.

Find 4 × 6.

Use an array.

Step 1

Use square tiles to make an array with 4 rows and 6 tiles in each row.

Step 2

Count the total number of tiles in the array to find the product.

There are _____ tiles in the array.

So, 4 × 6 = _____.

Find 5 × 6.

Use a number line.

Skip-count by sixes 5 times.

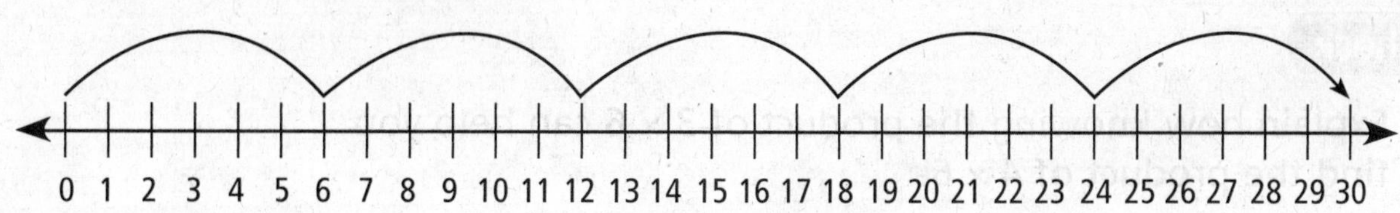

So, 5 × 6 = _____.

Do the Math

Use the array. Find the product.

1. 6 × 4 = ____

2. 6 × 5 = ____

3. 6 × 7 = ____

4. 6 × 2 = ____

Use the number line. Find the product.

5. 3 × 6 = ____

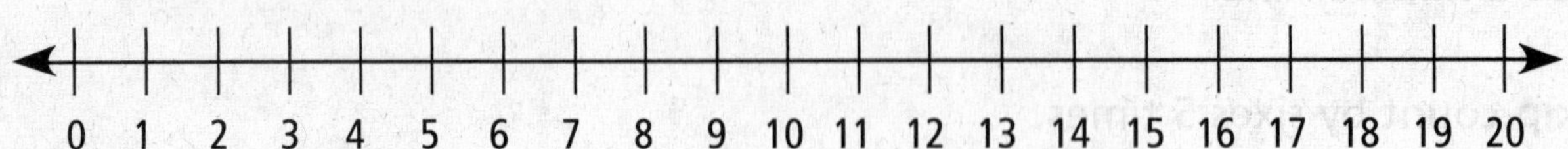

Check

6. Explain how knowing the product of 3 × 6 can help you find the product of 4 × 6.

____

____

____

Name ______________________________

Missing Factors
Skill 23

Learn the Math

You can use an array to find a missing factor.

Vocabulary

factor

Find the missing factor.
■ × 8 = 48

Step 1

Make an array with 48 tiles.

Put 8 tiles in each row.

Step 2

Count the number of rows.

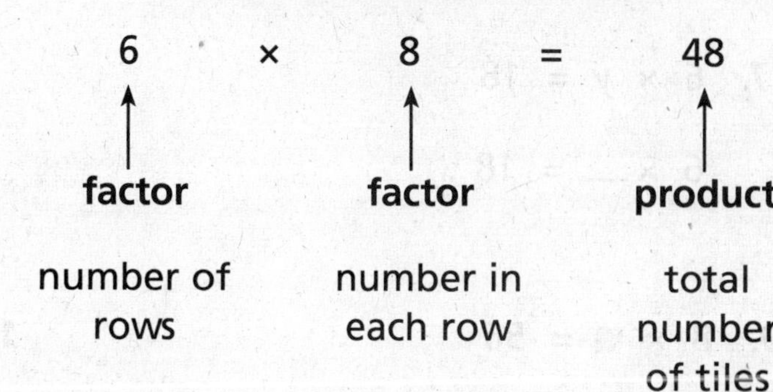

So, _____ × 8 = 48.

Find the missing factor.
7 × m = 35

Step 1

Make an array with _____ tiles. Make 7 rows.

Add one tile to each row until all 35 tiles

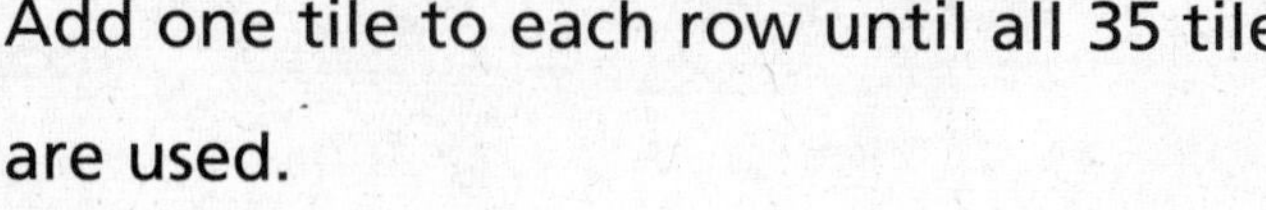

are used.

Step 2

Count the number of tiles in each row. There are _____ tiles in each row.

So, 7 × _____ = 35.

Find the missing factor.

1. $4 \times ■ = 16$

$4 \times \_\_\_ = 16$

2. $■ \times 5 = 25$

$\_\_\_ \times 5 = 25$

3. $8 \times a = 56$

$8 \times \_\_\_ = 56$

4. $6 \times b = 30$

$6 \times \_\_\_ = 30$

5. $7 \times ■ = 21$

$7 \times \_\_\_ = 21$

6. $■ \times 8 = 16$

$\_\_\_ \times 8 = 16$

7. $6 \times y = 18$

$6 \times \_\_\_ = 18$

8. $z \times 9 = 45$

$\_\_\_ \times 9 = 45$

9. $8 \times ■ = 56$

$8 \times \_\_\_ = 56$

10. $■ \times 6 = 24$

$\_\_\_ \times 6 = 24$

Check

11. If the first factor in a multiplication sentence is 5 and the product is 20, what array would you use to find the missing factor? What is the missing factor? Draw an array. Write the multiplication sentence.

$\_\_\_\_ \times \_\_\_\_ = \_\_\_\_$

Name ______________________________

Multiplicaton Facts Through 10

Skill 25

Learn the Math

You can use different strategies to find a product.

Find 3 × 5.

Use a multiplication table.

×	0	1	2	3	4	5	6	7	8	9	10
0	0	0	0	0	0	0	0	0	0	0	0
1	0	1	2	3	4	5	6	7	8	9	10
2	0	2	4	6	8	10	12	14	16	18	20
3	0	3	6	9	12	15	18	21	24	27	30
4	0	4	8	12	16	20	24	28	32	36	40
5	0	5	10	15	20	25	30	35	40	45	50
6	0	6	12	18	24	30	36	42	48	54	60
7	0	7	14	21	28	35	42	49	56	63	70
8	0	8	16	24	32	40	48	56	64	72	80
9	0	9	18	27	36	45	54	63	72	81	90
10	0	10	20	30	40	50	60	70	80	90	100

Find where the row for 3 and the column for 5 meet.

3 × 5 = _____

Make an array.

Count the tiles.
3 rows of 5 tiles

3 × 5 = _____

Draw a picture.

Show 3 groups of 5.

3 × 5 = _____

Use a number line.

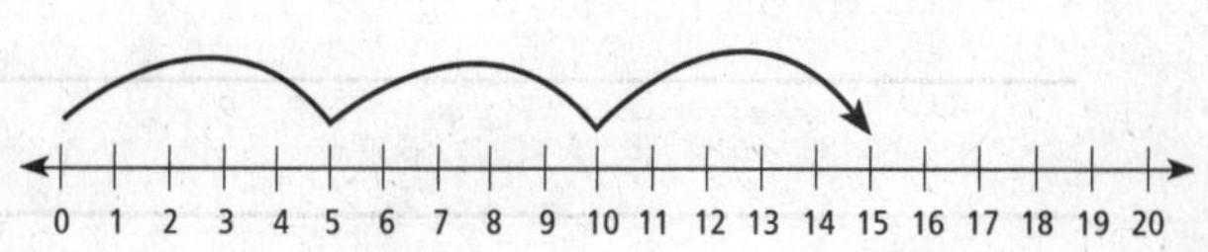

Make 3 jumps of 5 spaces each.

3 × 5 = _____

Do the Math

Find the product.

1. 7 × 8 = _____

2. 5 × 6 = _____

3. 4 × 4 = _____

4. 3 × 7 = _____

5. 6 × 8 = _____

6. 5 × 1 = _____

7. 3 × 8

8. 9 × 4

9. 10 × 3

10. 8 × 5

11. 3 × 9

12. 6 × 4

13. 6 × 6

14. 10 × 2

15. 5 × 4

Check

16. Look back at Problem 4. Explain how to find the answer. Draw a picture if necessary.

____

____

____

Name____________________

Multiplication Properties
Skill 26

Learn the Math

You can use multiplication properties to help you find products.

Vocabulary

Associative Property
Commutative Property
Identity Property
Zero Property

Identity Property

The product of 1 and any number equals that number.

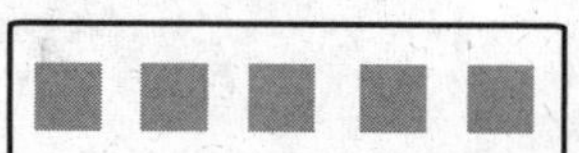

1 × 5 = 5

Zero Property

The product of 0 and any number equals 0.

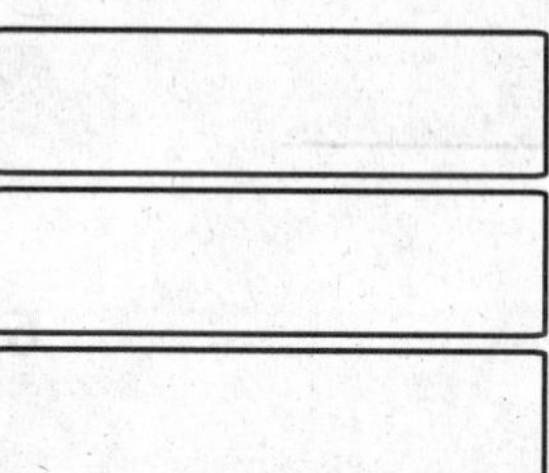

3 × 0 = 0

Commutative Property

You can multiply two factors in any order and get the same product.

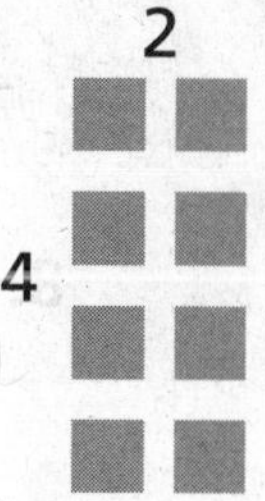

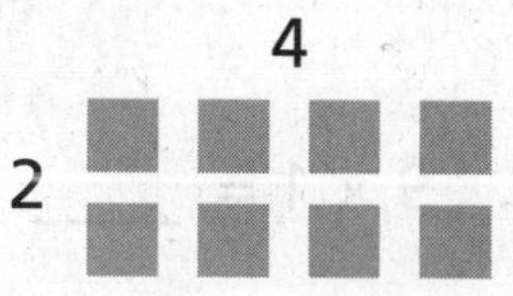

4 × 2 = 8

2 × 4 = ____

Associative Property

You can group factors in different ways and get the same product.

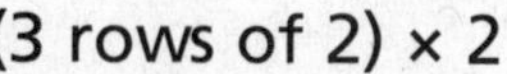
(3 rows of 2) × 2

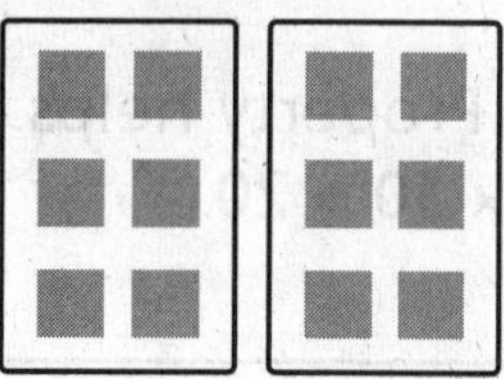

3 × (2 rows of 2)

(3 × 2) × 2 = ■

6 × 2 = 12

3 × (2 × 2) = ■

3 × 4 = ____

Do the Math

Find the product. Tell which property you used to help you.

1. 1 × 6 = ____

____

2. 5 × 0 = ____

____

3. 9 × 2 = ____

 2 × 9 = ____

____

4. 10 × 1 = ____

____

5. (2 × 3) × 3 = ____

 2 × (3 × 3) = ____

____

6. 4 × (2 × 5) = ____

 (4 × 2) × 5 = ____

____

7. 9 × 1 = ____

____

8. 8 × 7 = ____

 7 × 8 = ____

____

Check

9. Explain how the Commutative Property helps you find 10 … when you know that 2 × 10 = 20.

____

____

____

IIN51 • Tier 3

Name______________________________

Practice Multiplication Facts

Skill 27

Learn the Math

Use the multiplication strategies and properties you have learned to practice multiplication facts.

Multiplication Strategies

Use a multiplication table.

×	0	1	2	3	4	5	6	7	8	9	10
0	0	0	0	0	0	0	0	0	0	0	0
1	0	1	2	3	4	5	6	7	8	9	10
2	0	2	4	6	8	10	12	14	16	18	20
3	0	3	6	9	12	15	18	21	24	27	30
4	0	4	8	12	16	20	24	28	32	36	40
5	0	5	10	15	20	25	30	35	40	45	50
6	0	6	12	18	24	30	36	42	48	54	60
7	0	7	14	21	28	35	42	49	56	63	70
8	0	8	16	24	32	40	48	56	64	72	80
9	0	9	18	27	36	45	54	63	72	81	90
10	0	10	20	30	40	50	60	70	80	90	100

2 × 3 = _____

Draw a picture.

4 × 3 = _____

Make an array.

2 × 5 = _____

Use a number line.

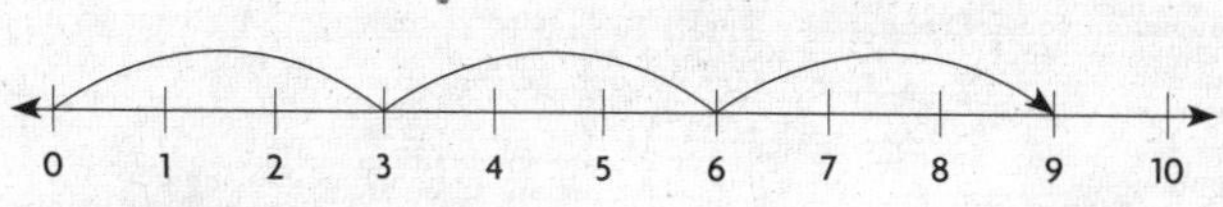

3 × 3 = _____

Multiplication Properties

Identity Property

The product of 1 and any number equals that number.

1 × 4 = _____

Zero Property

The product of 0 and any number equals 0.

4 × 0 = _____

Commutative Property

You can multiply two factors in any order and get the same product.

2 × 5 = _____

5 × 2 = _____

Associative Property

You can group factors in different ways and get the same product.

(4 × 2) × 3 = _____ 4 × (2 × 3) = _____

8 × 3 = _____ 4 × 6 = _____

Do the Math

Find each product.

1. 1 × 8 = ____

2. 6 × 0 = ____

3. 3 × (4 × 2) = ____

   (3 × 4) × 2 = ____

4. (6 × 2) × 3 = ____

   6 × (2 × 3) = ____

5. 9 × 5 = ____

   5 × 9 = ____

6. 10 × 4 = ____

   4 × 10 = ____

7. 8 × 5

8. 1 × 0

9. 2 × 9

10. 4 × 7

11. 8 × 6

12. 3 × 4

13. 5 × 7

14. 7 × 1

Check

15. Look back at Problem 8. How did you find the product?

______

______

______

Name ____________________

Model Multiplication by 1-Digit Numbers

Skill 28

Learn the Math

You can use models to multiply two-digit numbers by one-digit numbers.

Find 16 × 2.

Step 1

Use base-ten blocks to model 2 groups of 16.

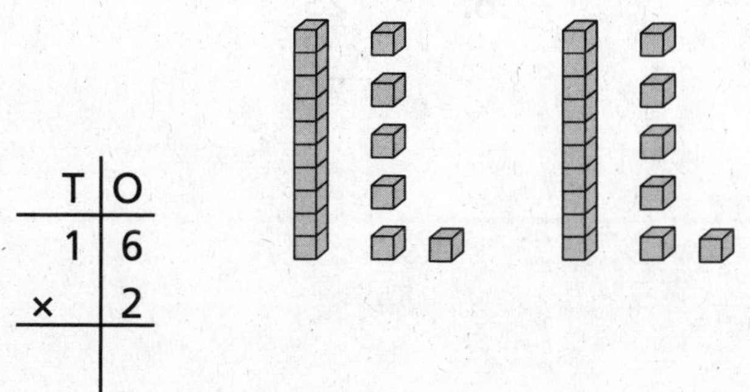

Step 2

Multiply the ones. (2 × 6 ones)

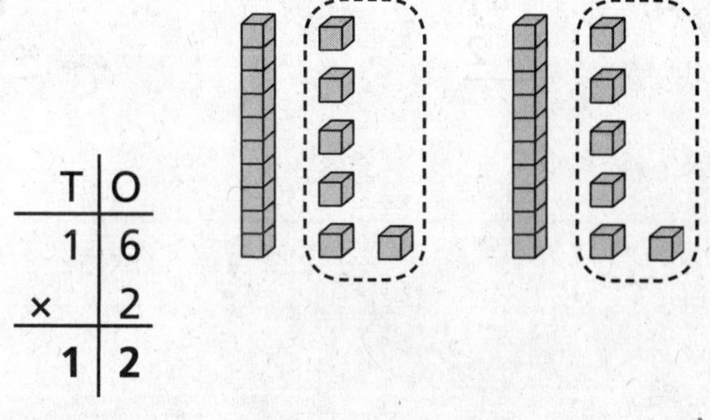

Step 3

Multiply the tens. (2 × 1 ten)

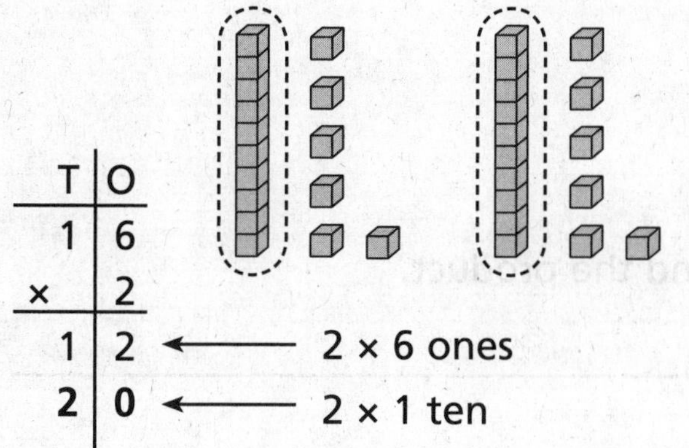

Step 4

Add to find the product.

	T	O
	1	6
×		2
	1	2
+	2	0
	3	**2**

So, 16 × 2 = ______.

Do the Math

Multiply. You may wish to use base-ten blocks to help you. Show your work.

1. $\begin{array}{r} 27 \\ \times\ 2 \\ \hline \end{array}$

2. $\begin{array}{r} 32 \\ \times\ 1 \\ \hline \end{array}$

3. $\begin{array}{r} 18 \\ \times\ 2 \\ \hline \end{array}$

4. $\begin{array}{r} 41 \\ \times\ 2 \\ \hline \end{array}$

5. $\begin{array}{r} 12 \\ \times\ 1 \\ \hline \end{array}$

6. $\begin{array}{r} 25 \\ \times\ 3 \\ \hline \end{array}$

7. $\begin{array}{r} 19 \\ \times\ 3 \\ \hline \end{array}$

8. $\begin{array}{r} 26 \\ \times\ 3 \\ \hline \end{array}$

9. $\begin{array}{r} 41 \\ \times\ 3 \\ \hline \end{array}$

Check

10. Look back at Problem 3. Tell how to find the product.

____

____

____

____

Name ______________________

Round to the Nearest Ten

Skill 29

Learn the Math

You can use a number line or place value to round a number to the nearest ten.

Use a number line.

Round 126 to the nearest ten.

Step 1 Find 126 on the number line.

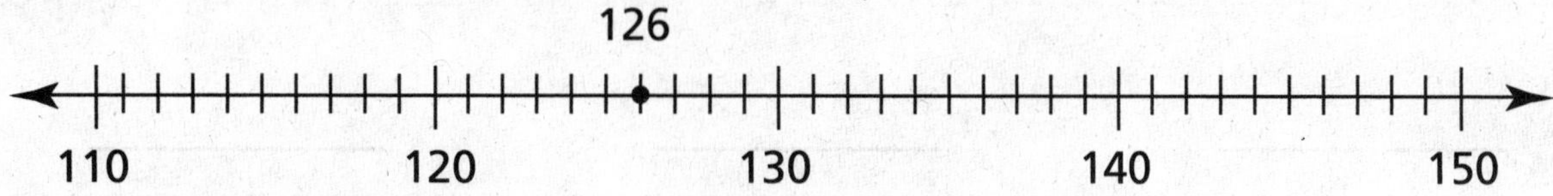

Step 2 Find the nearest ten on the number line.
126 is closer to 130 than to 120.

So, 126 rounded to the nearest ten is **130**.

Use place value.

Round 532 to the nearest ten.

Step 1 Find the place to which you want to round.

532 — 3 is in the tens place.

Step 2 Look at the digit to the right.

53<u>2</u> — If the digit is less than 5, the digit in the rounding place stays the same. If the digit is 5 or greater, the digit in the rounding place increases by one.

Since 2 < 5, the tens digit stays the same.

Step 3 Change all the digits to the right of the rounding place to zero.

532 ⟶ 530

So, 532 rounded to the nearest ten is ______.

Do the Math

Round the number to the nearest ten.

1. 24 ___

2. 67 ___

3. 99 ___

4. 674 ___

5. 329 ___

6. 137 ___

7. 519 ___

8. 222 ___

9. 941 ___

10. 455 ___

11. 783 ___

12. 866 ___

Check

13. Explain how you would use place value to round 98 to the nearest ten.

___

___

___

___

Name____

Learn the Math

Plane figures have many different shapes.

triangle rhombus hexagon square

trapezoid circle rectangle parallelogram

Vocabulary

- circle
- hexagon
- parallelogram
- rectangle
- rhombus
- square
- trapezoid
- triangle

Circle the triangles. Cross out the figures that are NOT triangles.

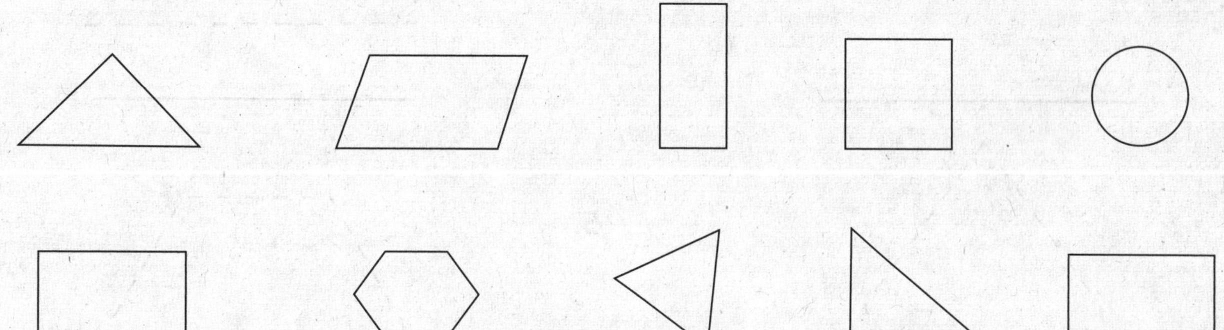

Trace each figure. Then write the name of the figure.

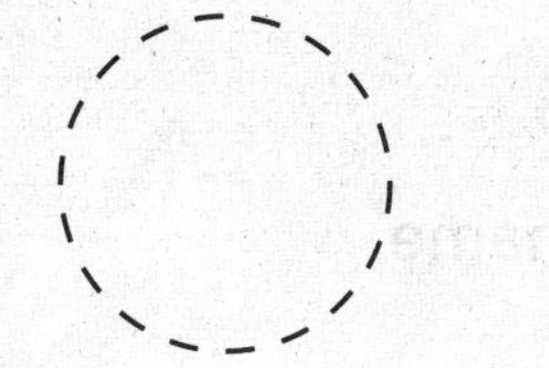

____________________ ____________________

Do the Math

Circle the squares. Cross out the figures that are NOT squares.

1.

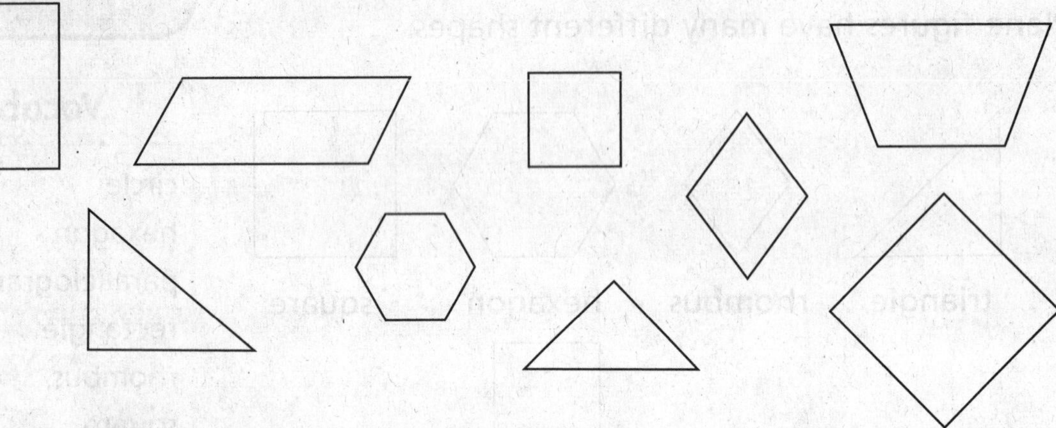

Trace each figure. Then write the name of the figure.

2.

____

3.

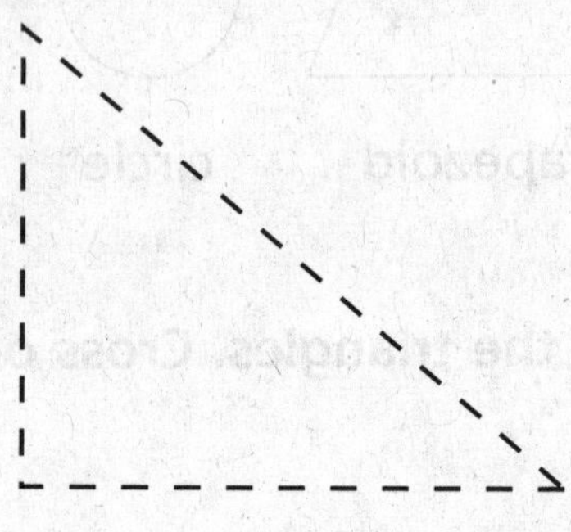

____

4.

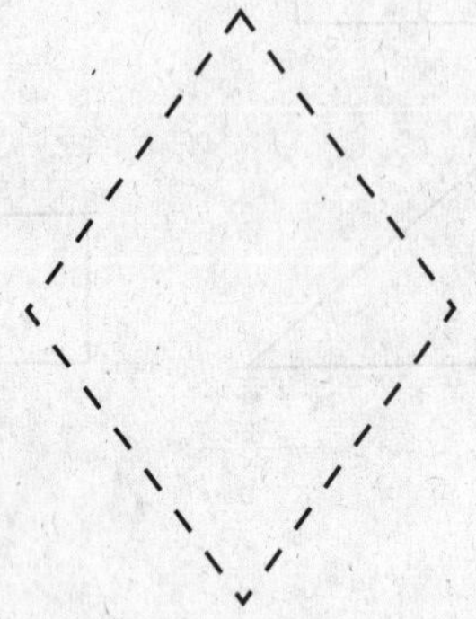

____

5.

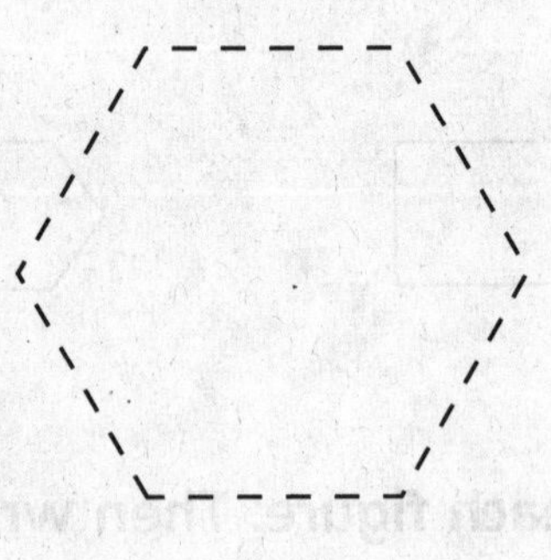

____

Check

6. Look back at Problem 3. How did you decide the name of the figure?

____

____

Name_______________________________________

Sides and Vertices

Skill 32

Learn the Math

Some figures have straight lines as sides that join at points called vertices.

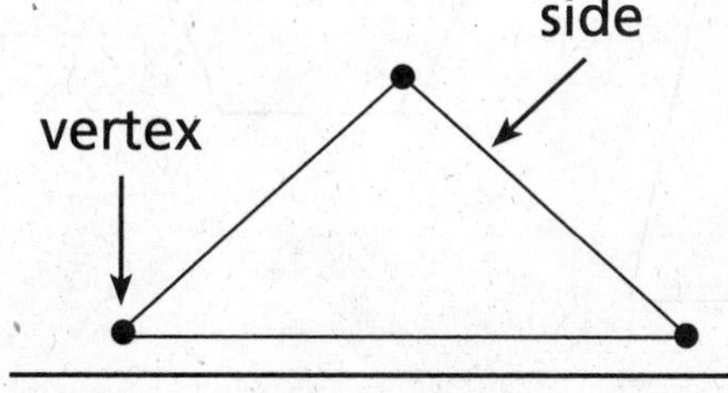

Vocabulary

side
vertex
vertices

Which figures have 4 sides and 4 vertices?

Count the number of sides each figure has.

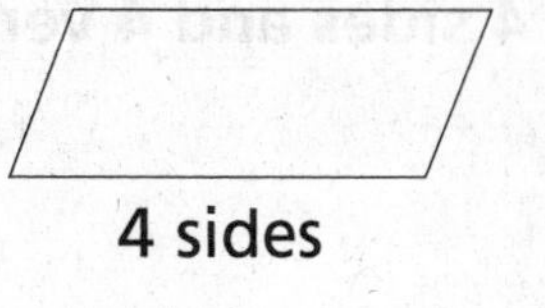
4 sides

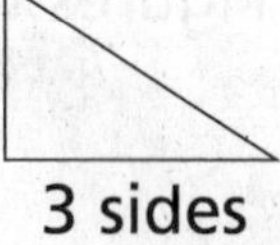
3 sides

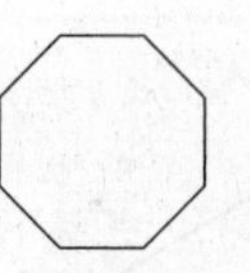
8 sides

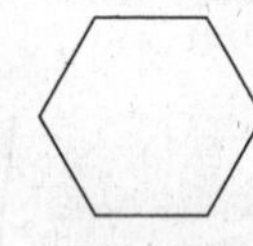
6 sides

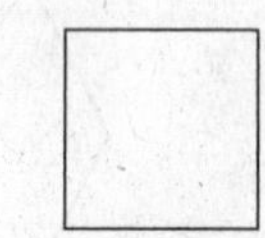
4 sides

Count the number of vertices each figure has.

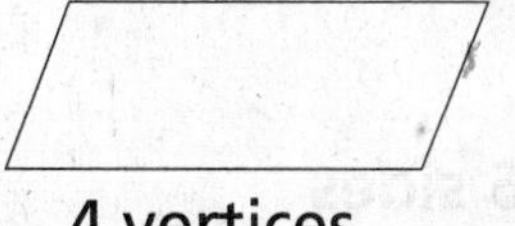
4 vertices

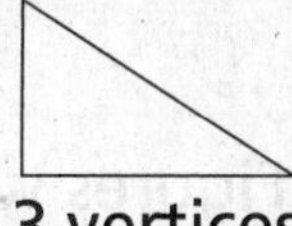
3 vertices

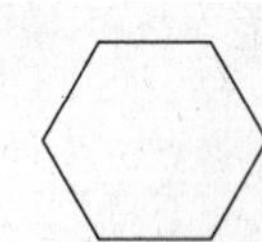
8 vertices

6 vertices

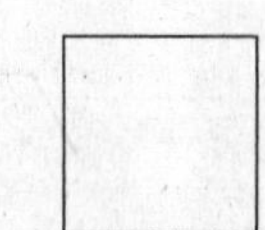
4 vertices

Cross out the figures that do not have 4 sides and 4 vertices. Identify the figures that do.

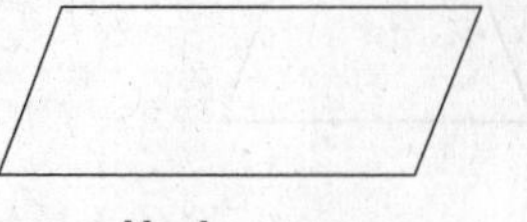
parallelogram

triangle

octagon

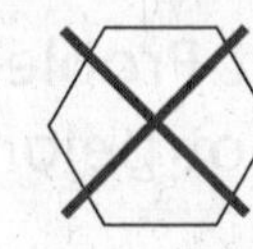
hexagon

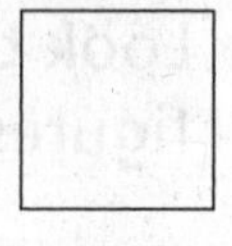
square

A ____________________ and a ____________________ have 4 sides and 4 vertices.

Cross out the figures that do NOT belong.

1. Figures with **3 vertices**

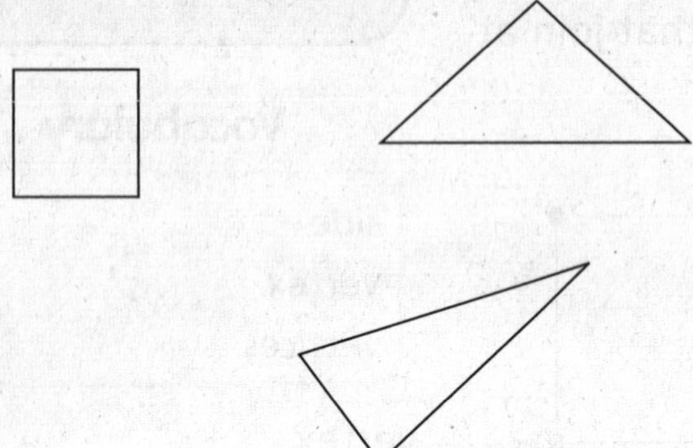

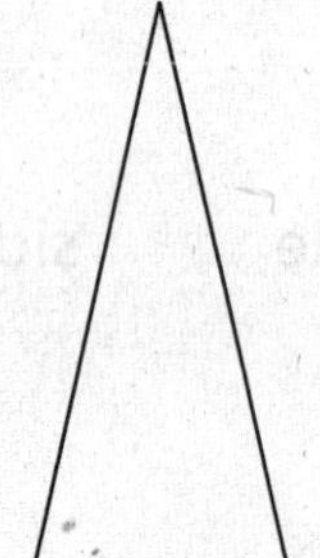

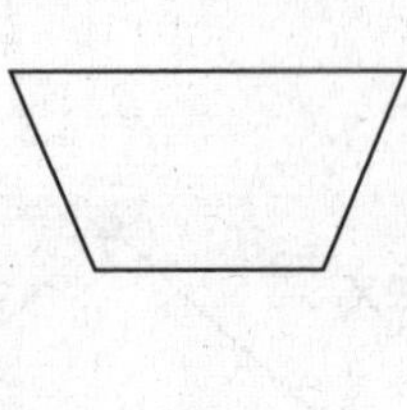

2. Figures with **4 sides and 4 vertices**

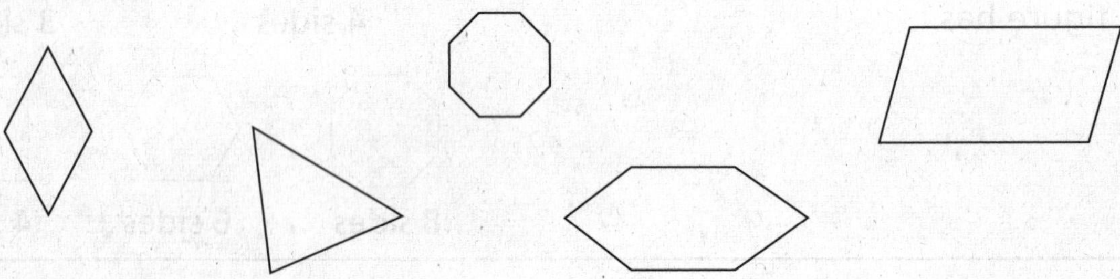

3. Figures with **6 sides**

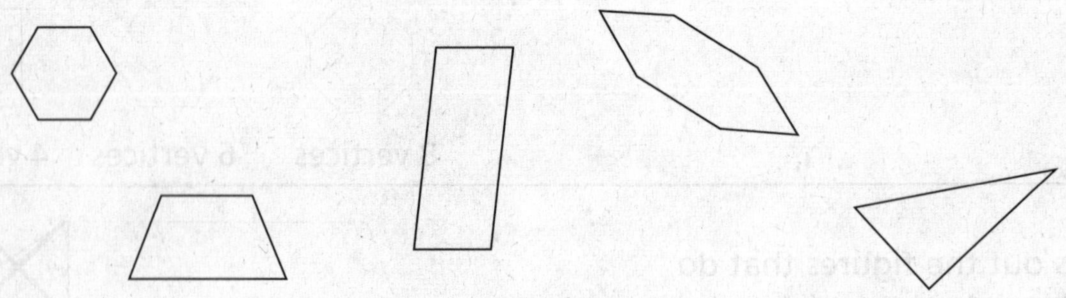

Check

4. Look back at Problem 2. Which figures belong in the group? Which figures do not belong in the group? How do you know?

____

____

____

Name______________________________

Learn the Math

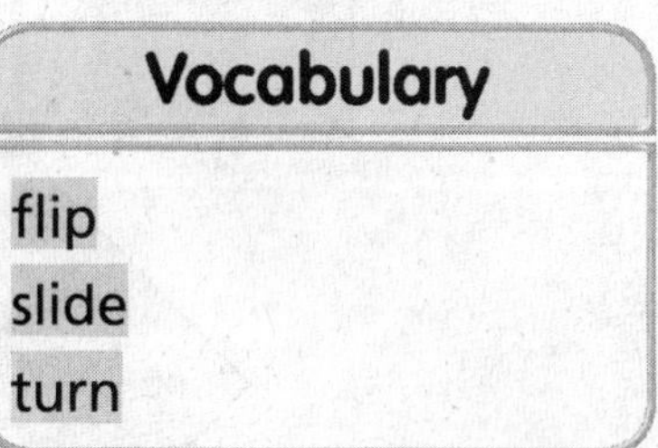

You can move figures different ways.

You can **slide** a figure.

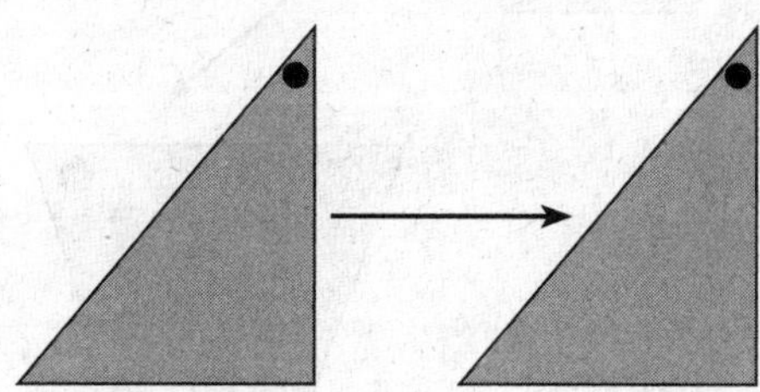

You can **flip** a figure across a line.

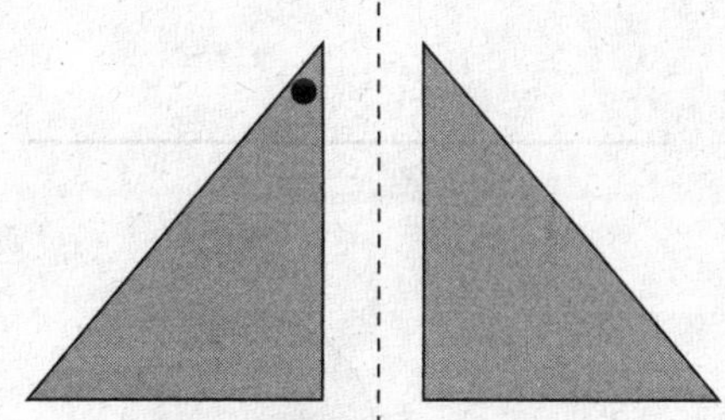

You can **turn** a figure around a point.

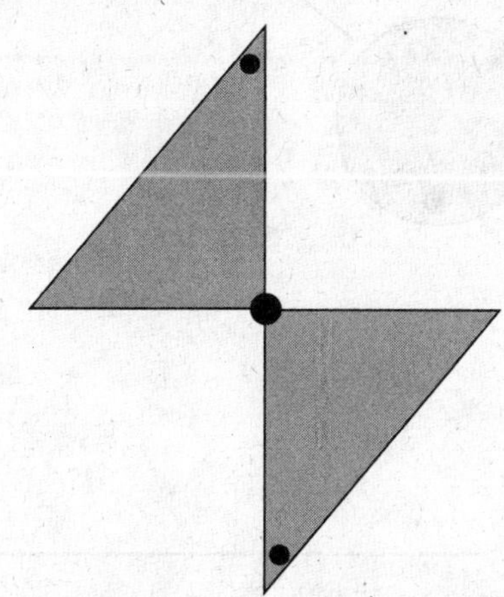

Describe how the figure has moved. Write *slide*, *flip*, or *turn*.

____

Describe how the figure has moved. Write *slide, flip,* or *turn*.

1.

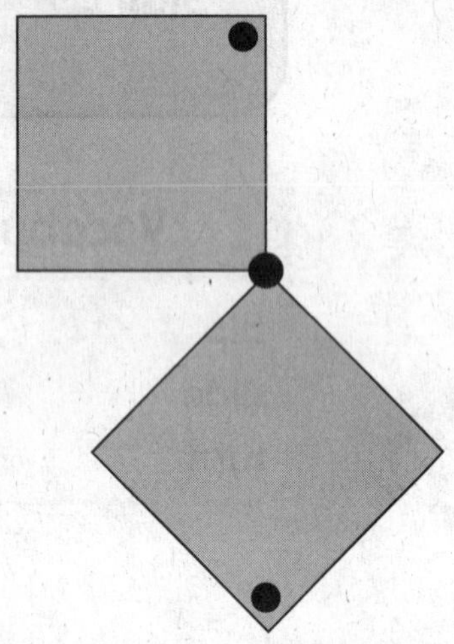

____

2.

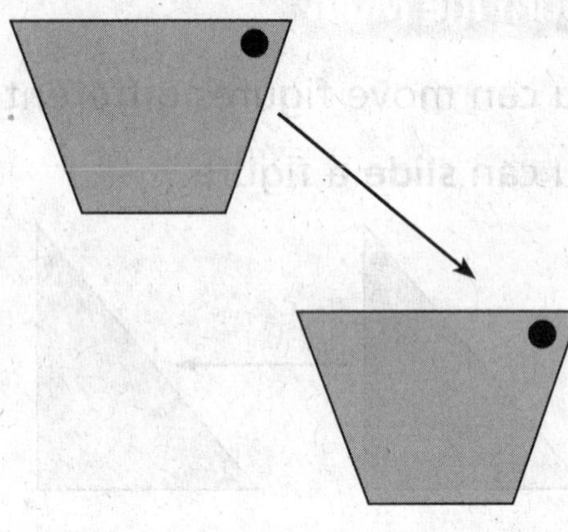

____

3.

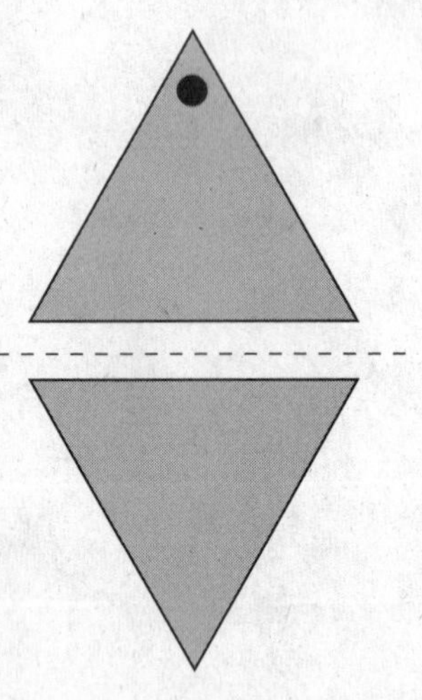

____

4.

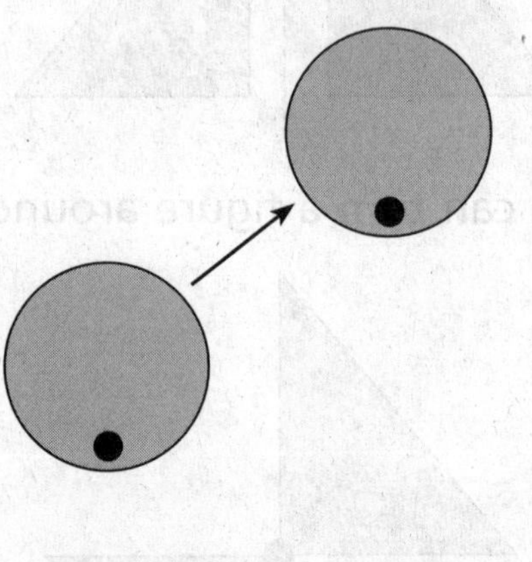

____

Check

5. Look back at Problem 4. How did you decide how the figure had moved?

____

____

____

Name________________________________

Learn the Math

Congruent figures have the same size and the same shape.

Vocabulary

congruent

The figures below have the same size and shape. They are congruent.

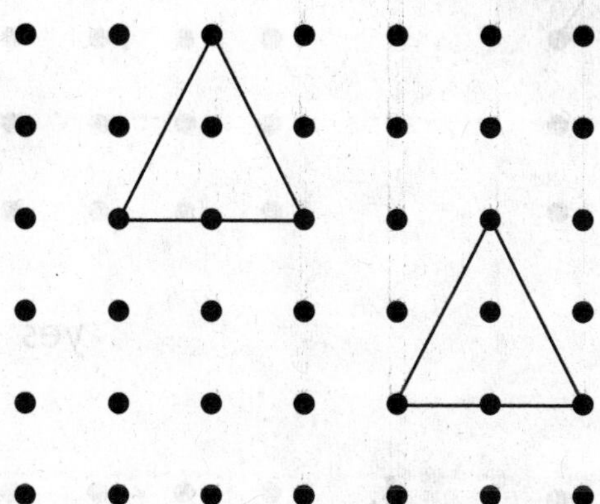

These figures are not the same size. They are not congruent.

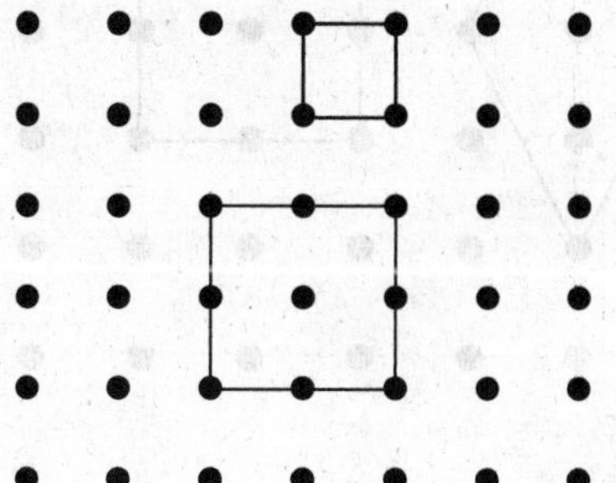

These figures are not the same shape. They are not congruent.

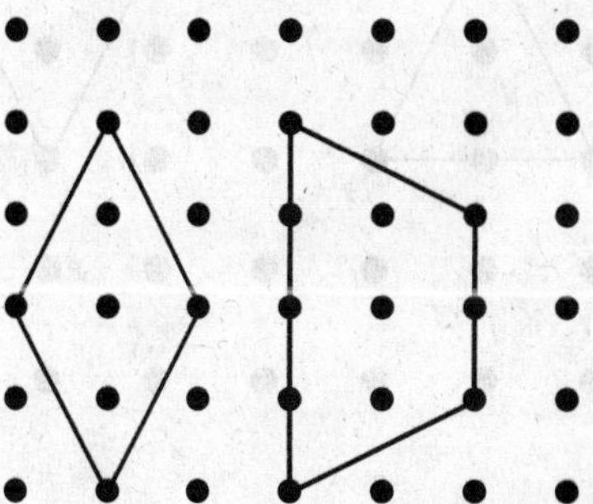

Are the two figures congruent? Circle *yes* or *no*.

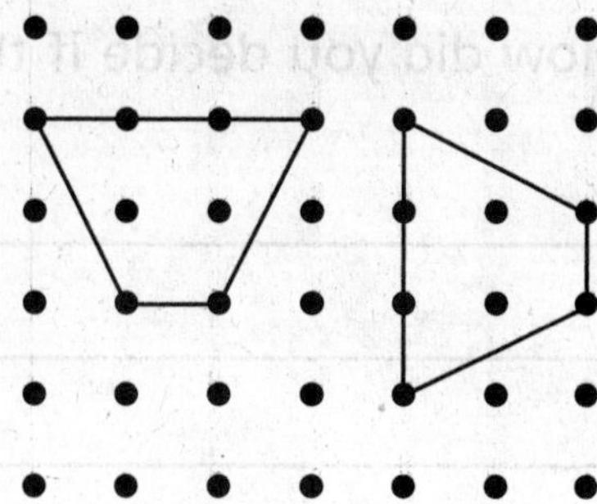

yes   no

Do the Math

Are the two figures congruent? Circle *yes* or *no*.

1.

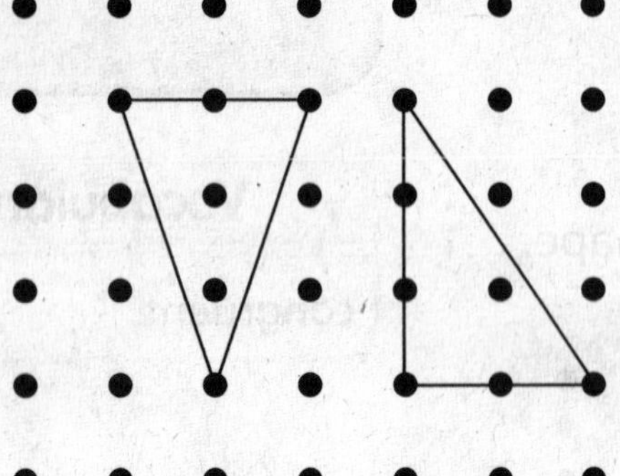

yes no

2.

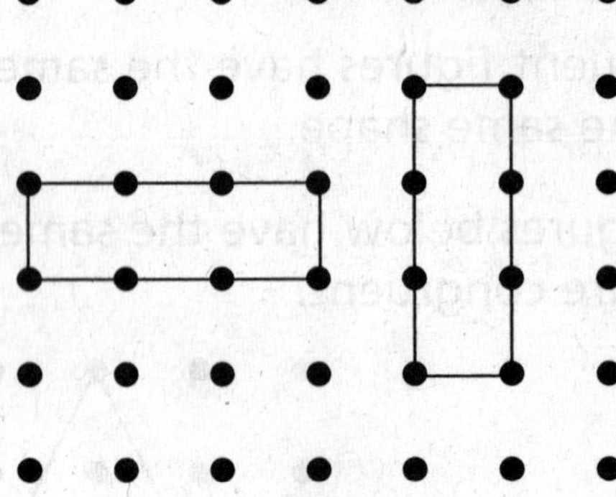

yes no

3.

yes no

4.

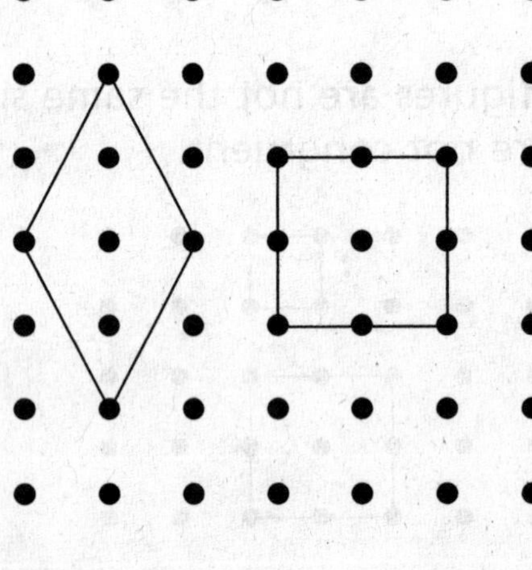

yes no

Check

5. Look back at Problem 2. How did you decide if the two figures are congruent?

Name____

Learn the Math

A figure has symmetry if it can be folded in half so that the halves match exactly. A line that divides a figure into two matching parts is a line of symmetry.

You can fold paper to explore symmetry. You will need paper, scissors, and a crayon or marker.

Vocabulary

symmetry
line of symmetry

Step 1

Fold the piece of paper in half.

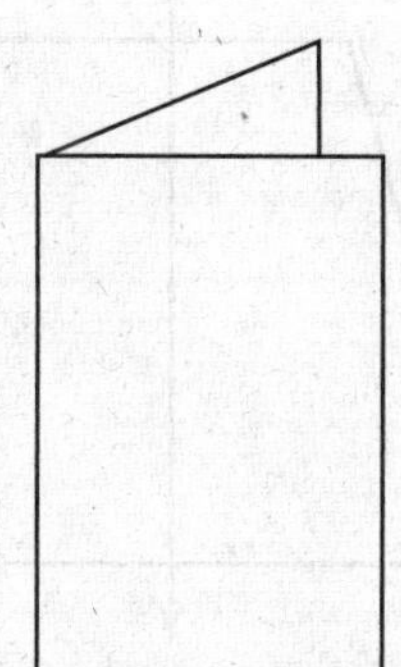

Step 2

Draw a figure that begins and ends on the fold.

Step 3

Cut out the figure with the paper still folded.

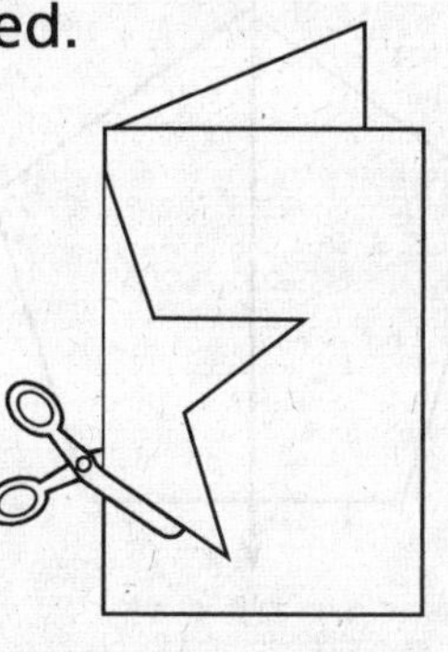

Step 4

Unfold the figure. Draw a line where the fold was.

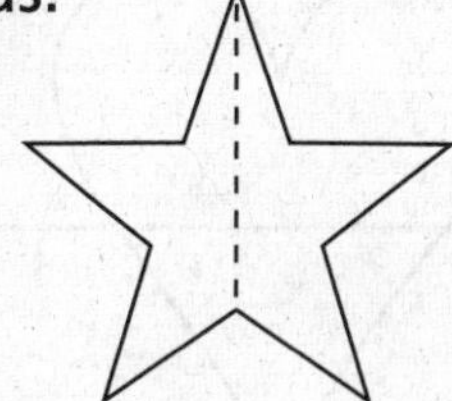

The fold is the line of symmetry.

Tell whether the line appears to be a line of symmetry. Write *yes* or *no*.

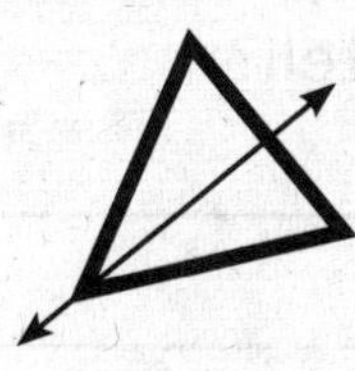

____

____

Do the Math

Tell whether the line appears to be a line of symmetry. Write *yes* or *no*.

1.

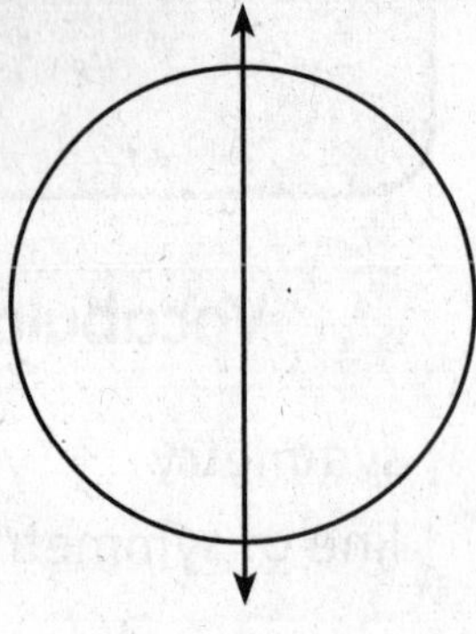

______

2.

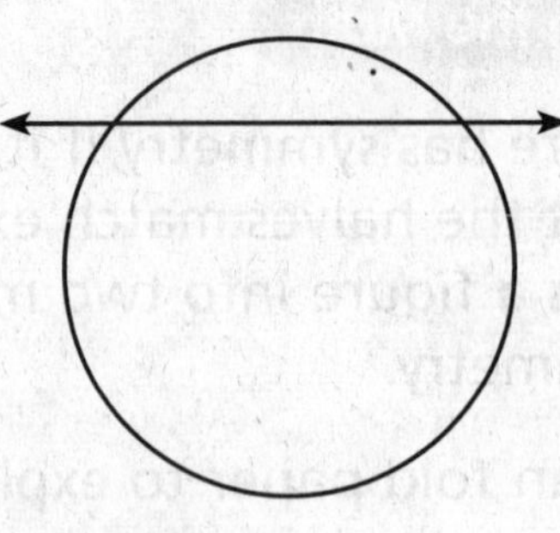

______

3.

______

4.

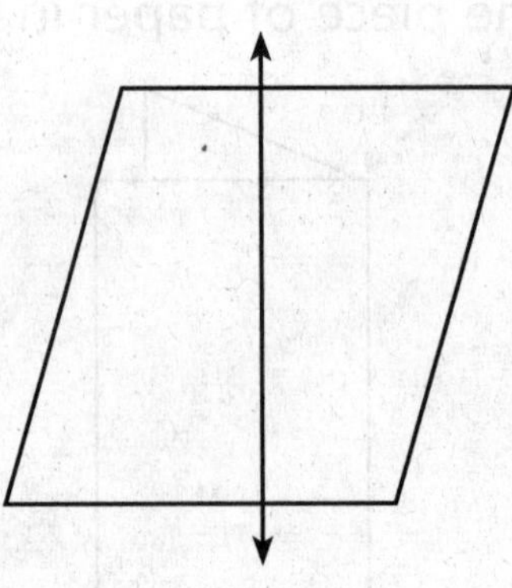

______

5.

______

6.

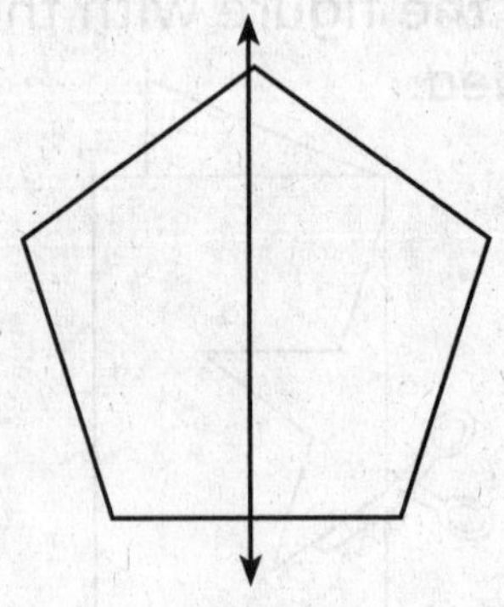

______

Check

7. Does this figure have symmetry? How can you tell?

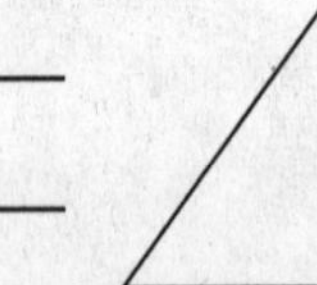

____

____

Name ______________________________

Solid Figures

Skill 36

Learn the Math

You can use names of solid figures to describe objects around you.

Vocabulary

cone
cube
cylinder
pyramid
rectangular prism
solid figure
sphere

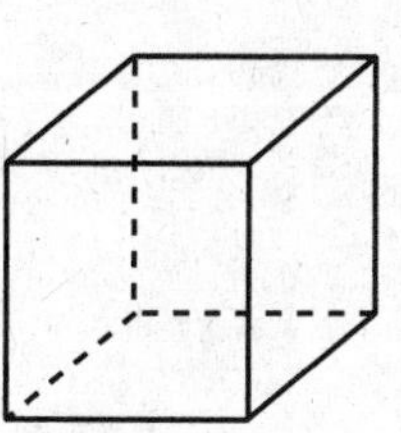

cube

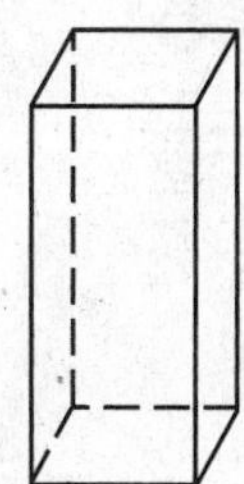

rectangular prism

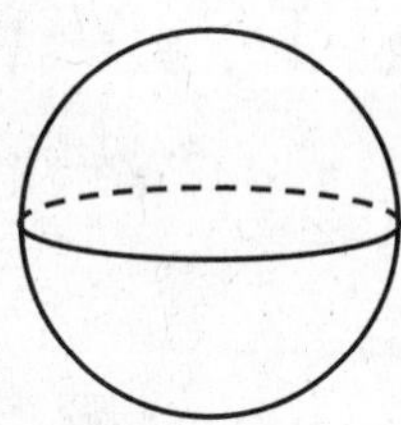

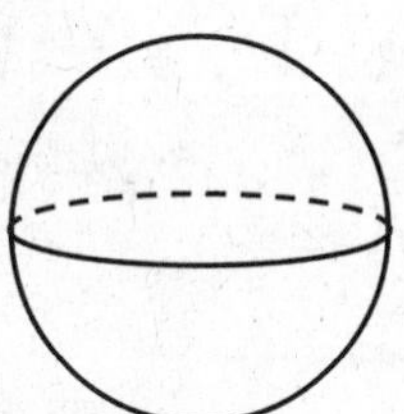

sphere

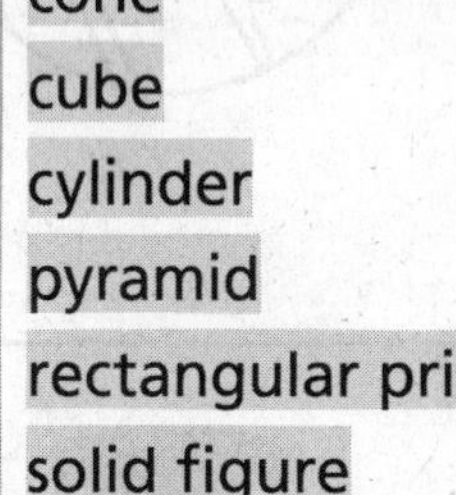

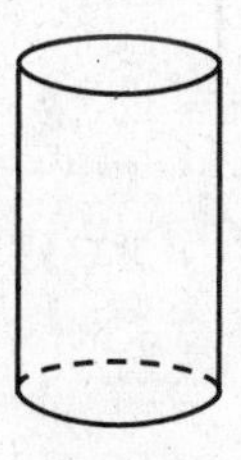

cylinder

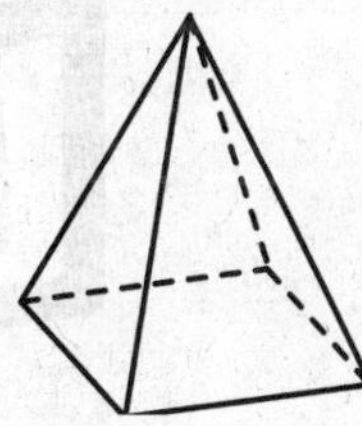

square pyramid

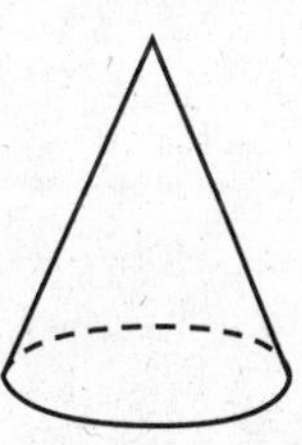

cone

Which solid figure is this hat shaped like?

Think: Does it have a flat surface? _____

Does it have a point? _____

Does it have a curved surface? _____

Look at the solid figures above.
Which figure does the hat look like? ____________

So, the hat is shaped like a ____________.

Do the Math

Name the solid figure that each object is shaped like.

1.

____

2.

____

3.

____

4.

____

5.

____

6.

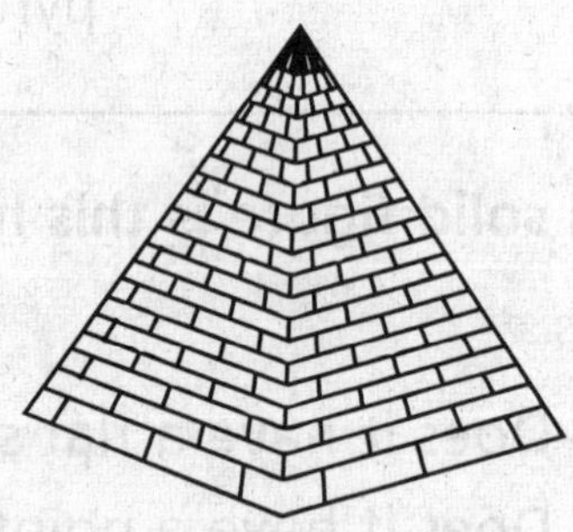

____

Check

7. Name a real world example of each solid figure.

cube ______________ sphere ______________

cone ______________ cylinder ______________

rectangular prism ______________ square pyramid ______________

Name____________________________________

Faces, Edges, Vertices

Skill 37

Learn the Math

You can describe a solid figure by the number of faces, edges, and vertices it has.

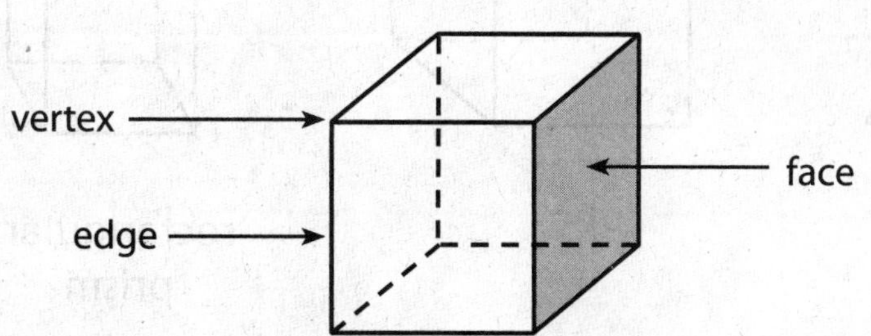

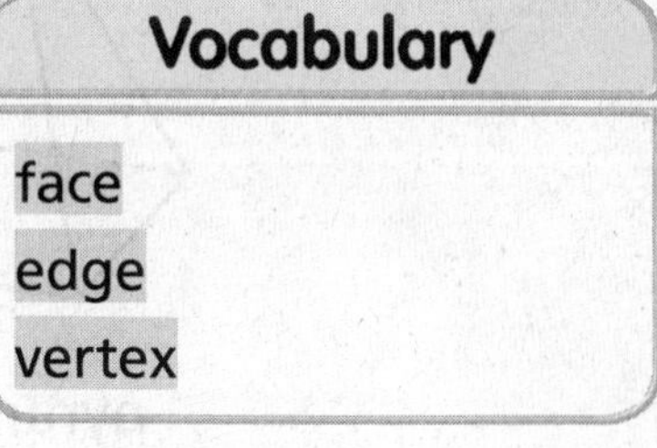

A **face** is a flat surface of a solid figure.

Shade a face of each figure.

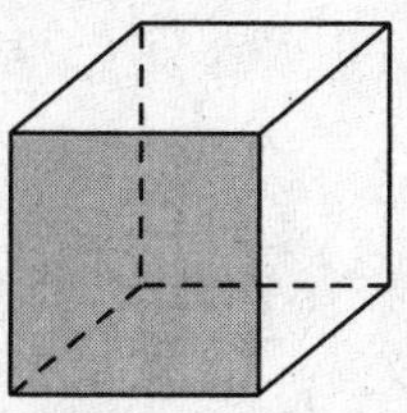

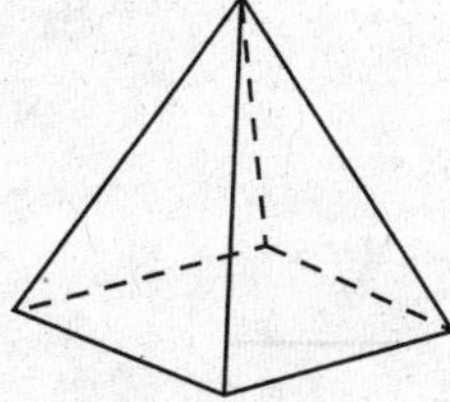

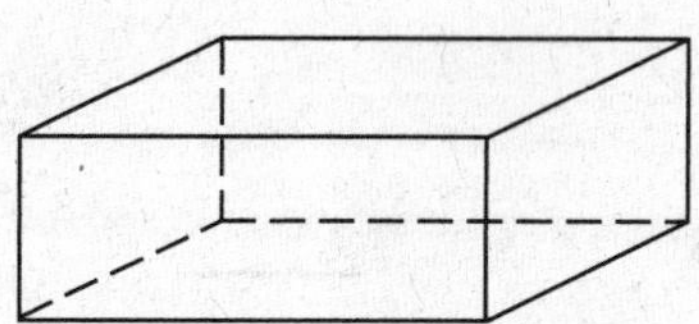

An **edge** is formed where two faces meet.

Put an X on an edge of each figure.

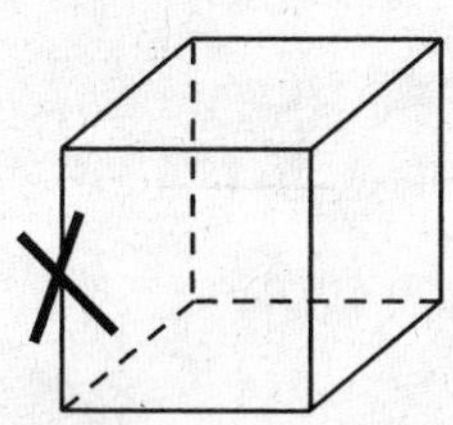

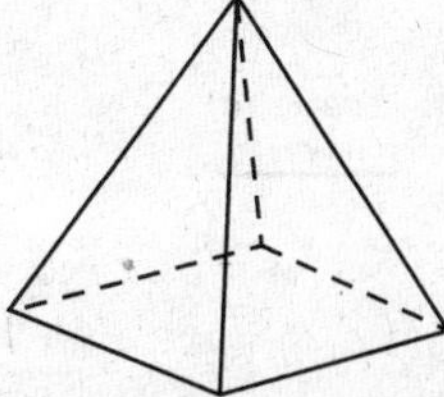

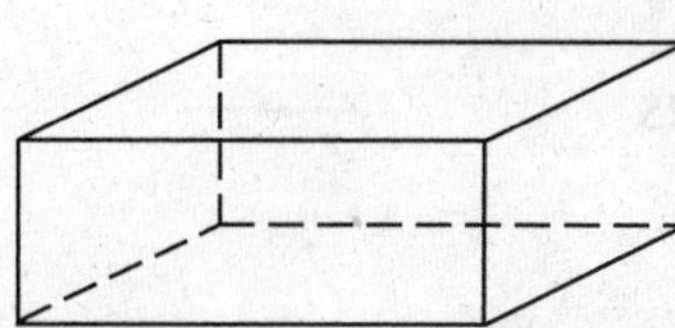

A **vertex** is a point where three or more edges meet.

Put a point on a vertex of each figure.

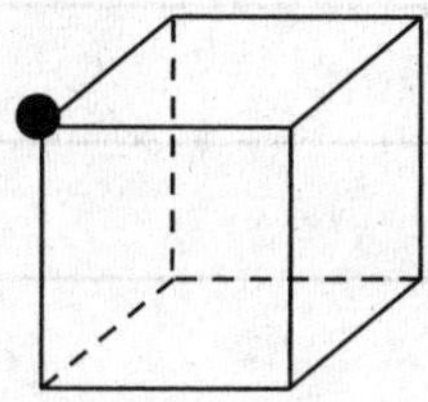

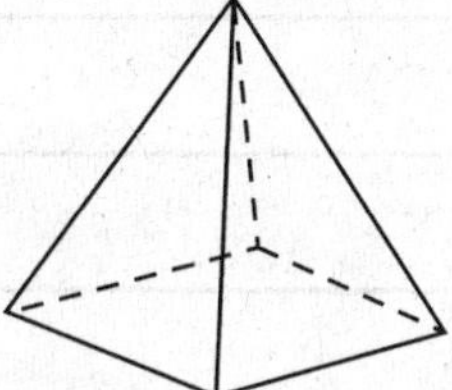

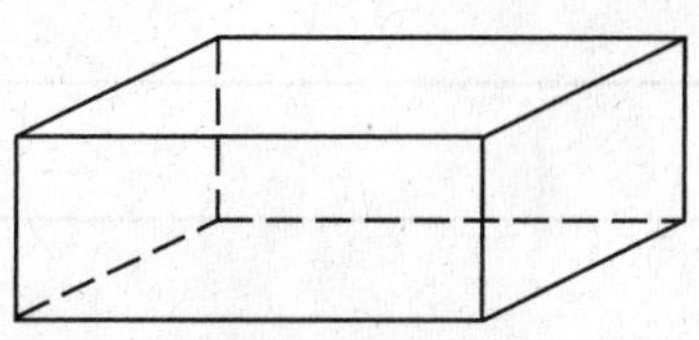

Do the Math

Write the number of faces, edges, and vertices for each solid figure.

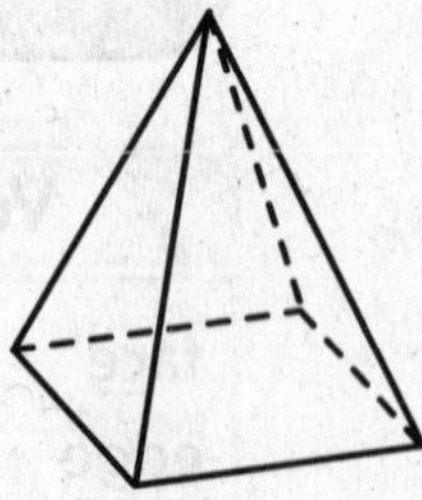

pyramid

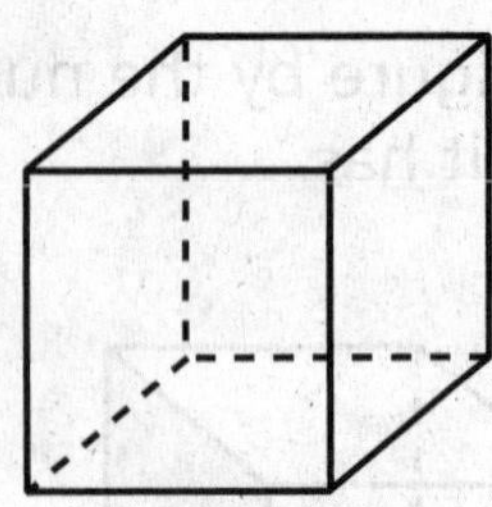

cube

rectangular prism

	pyramid	cube	rectangular prism
1. faces	____	____	____
2. edges	____	____	____
3. vertices	____	____	____

Check

4. Explain how a rectangular prism and a cube are alike and how they are different.

____

____

____

Name ___________________________

Use Arrays to Divide
Skill 38

Learn the Math

When you divide, you separate into equal groups. You can use arrays to find equal groups.

Vocabulary

array
divide

Divide. 28 ÷ 7

Step 1

Think: What number are you dividing? ____

So, count out 28 tiles.

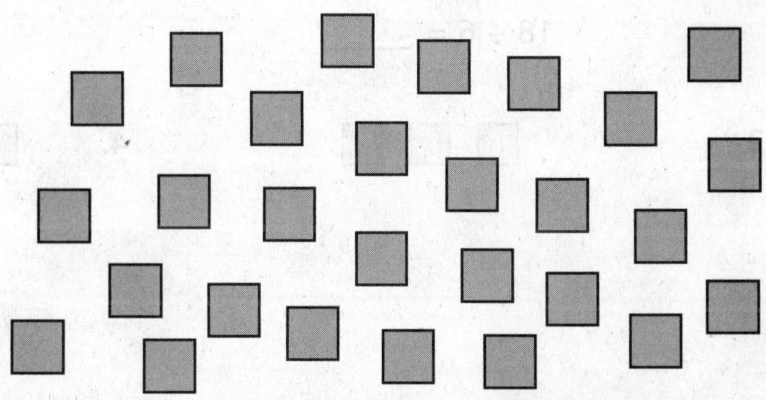

Step 2

Think: What number are you dividing by? ____

So, make a row of 7 tiles.

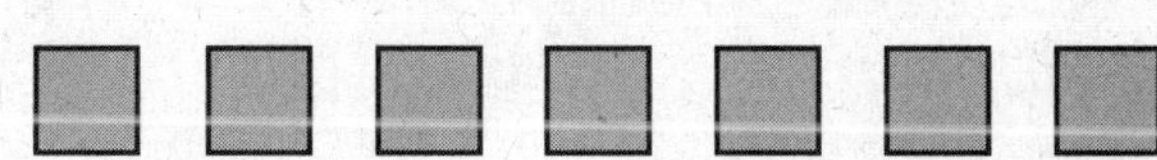

Continue to make rows of 7 tiles until all 28 tiles have been used.

Step 3

Count the number of rows you have made.

There are ____ rows of 7 tiles.

So, 28 ÷ 7 = ____ .

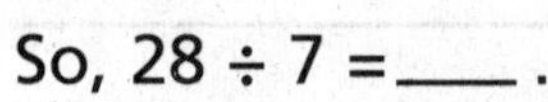

Draw to complete each array. Then complete the number sentence.

1. 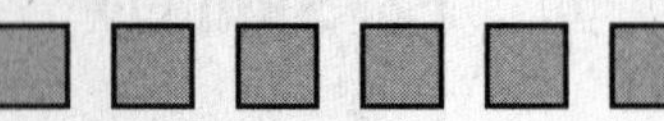

$18 \div 6 =$ _____

2.

$20 \div 5 =$ _____

3. 

$12 \div 3 =$ _____

4. 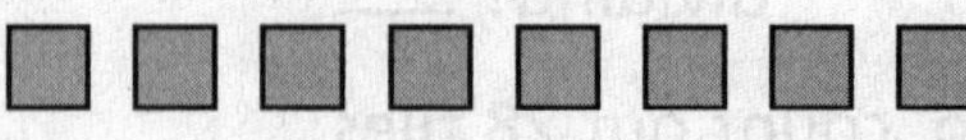

$24 \div 8 =$ _____

5. 

$25 \div 5 =$ _____

6. 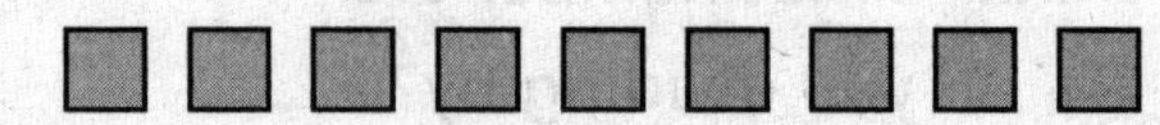

$45 \div 9 =$ _____

Check

7. How would you use tiles to model $16 \div 4$?

____

____

____

Name ____________________

Relate Division and Subtraction

Skill 39

Learn the Math

Vocabulary

divide

Subtracting equal groups is one way to divide.

Use models to find 12 ÷ 3.

Start with 12 stars. Take away groups of 3 until all stars are used. Count the number of times you subtract 3.

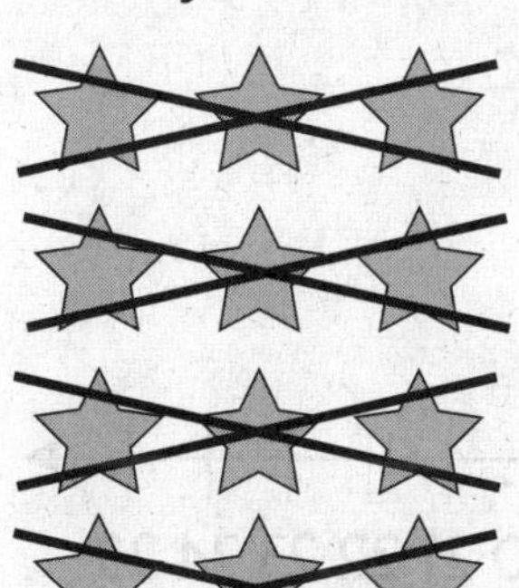

You subtract 3 four times. So, 12 ÷ 3 = _____.

Count back on a number line to find 16 ÷ 2.

Start at 16. Count back by 2s until you reach 0. Count the number of times you subtract 2.

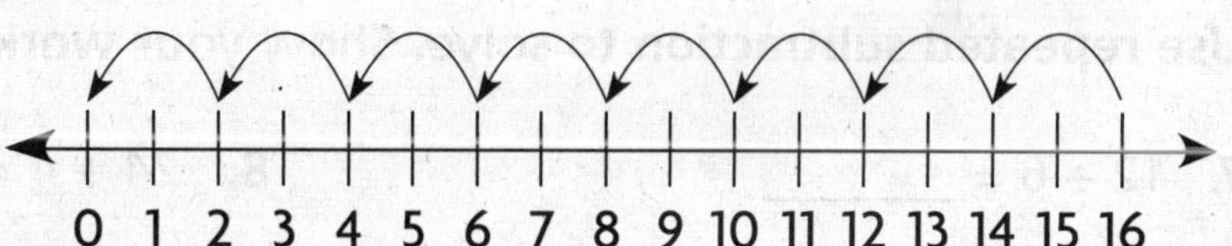

You subtract 2 eight times. So, 16 ÷ 2 = _____.

Use repeated subtraction to find 15 ÷ 5.

Start with 15. Subtract 5 until you reach 0. Count the number of times you subtract 5.

$$\begin{array}{r} 15 \\ -\ 5 \\ \hline 10 \end{array} \rightarrow \begin{array}{r} 10 \\ -\ 5 \\ \hline 5 \end{array} \rightarrow \begin{array}{r} 5 \\ -\ 5 \\ \hline 0 \end{array}$$

You subtract 5 three times. So, 15 ÷ 5 = _____.

Do the Math

Use a model to solve. Draw a picture to show your work.

1. 20 ÷ 5 = ________ **2.** 21 ÷ 3 = ________

Use a number line to solve.

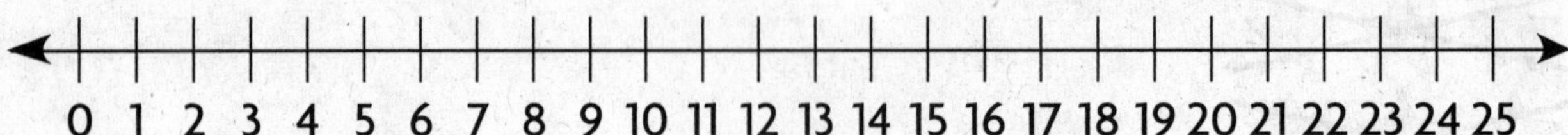

3. 18 ÷ 3 = ________ **4.** 24 ÷ 8 = ________

5. 14 ÷ 2 = ________ **6.** 9 ÷ 3 = ________

Use repeated subtraction to solve. Show your work.

7. 12 ÷ 6 = ________ **8.** 24 ÷ 4 = ________

Check

9. Explain how to use repeated subtraction to find 36 ÷ 9.

____

____

____

____

Name ______________________

Multiplication and Division Fact Families

Skill 40

Learn the Math

A fact family is a set of related multiplication and division number sentences.

Vocabulary

fact family

Fact Family for 3, 4, and 12

factor		factor		product	dividend		divisor		quotient
3	×	4	=	12	12	÷	4	=	3
4	×	3	=	12	12	÷	3	=	4

What fact family does the array below show?

columns

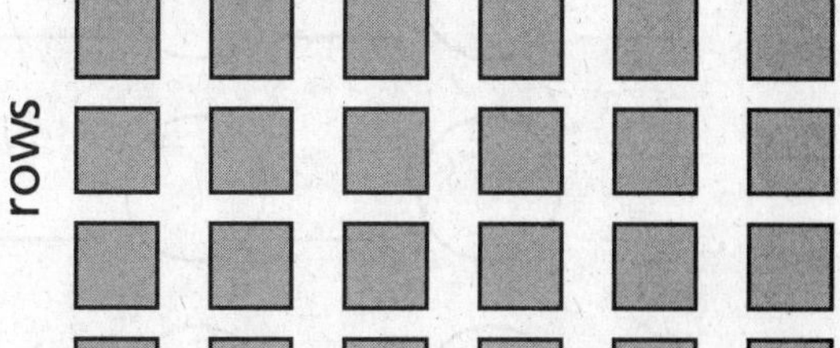

rows

Step 1 Count the number of rows.

There are ____ rows.

Step 2 Count the number of columns.

There are ____ columns.

Step 3 Count the total number of tiles.

There are ____ tiles.

Step 4 Write two multiplication sentences and two division sentences that describe the array.

Think: What multiplication and division facts use the numbers 5, 6, and 30?

5 × 6 = 30

6 × 5 = 30

30 ÷ 6 = 5

30 ÷ 5 = 6

So, the fact family is

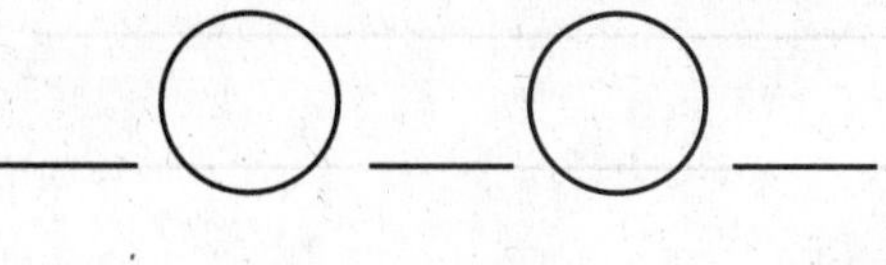

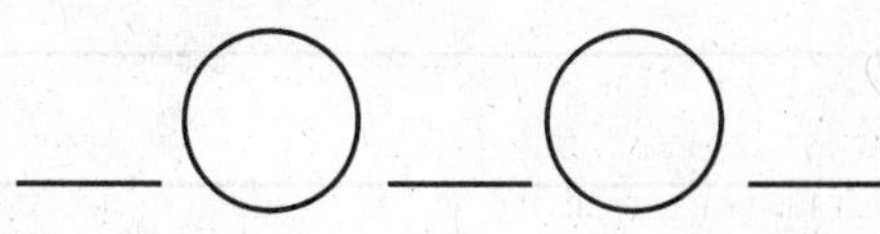

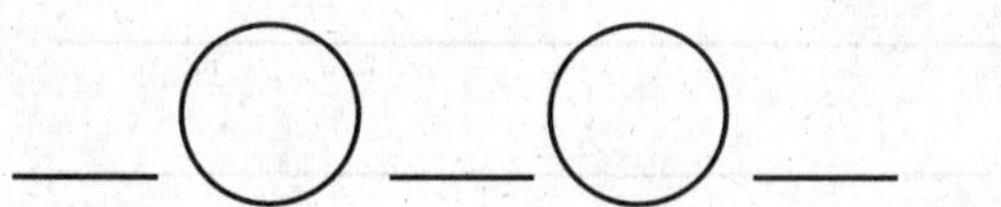

___ ◯ ___ ◯ ___

Write the fact family for each set of numbers.

1. 4, 5, 20

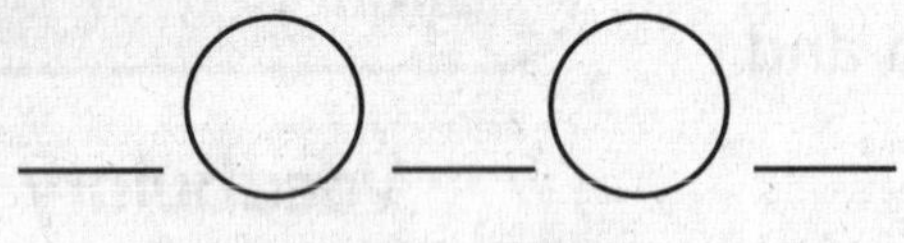

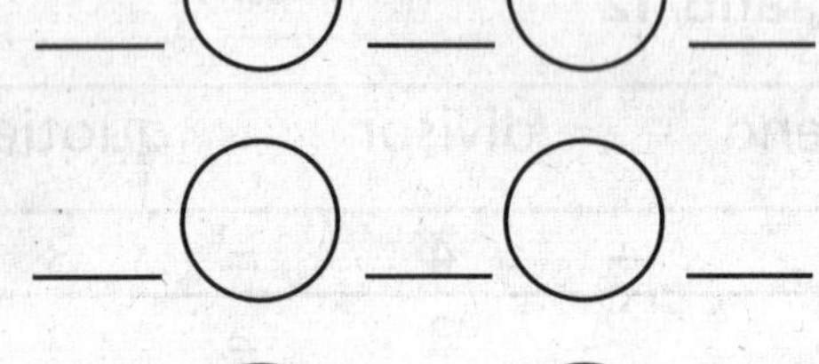

2. 3, 6, 18

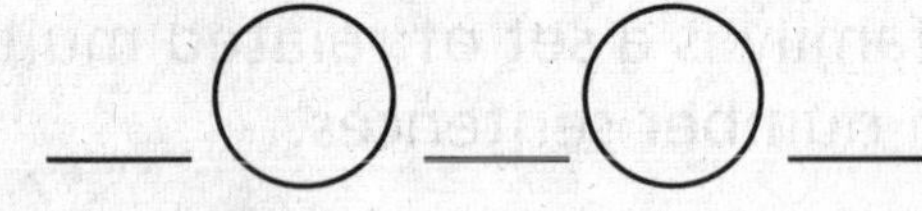

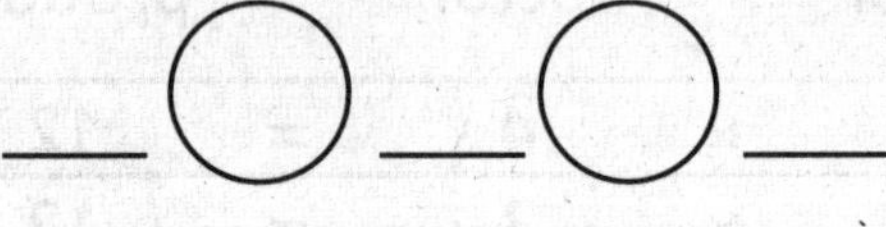

3. 2, 7, 14

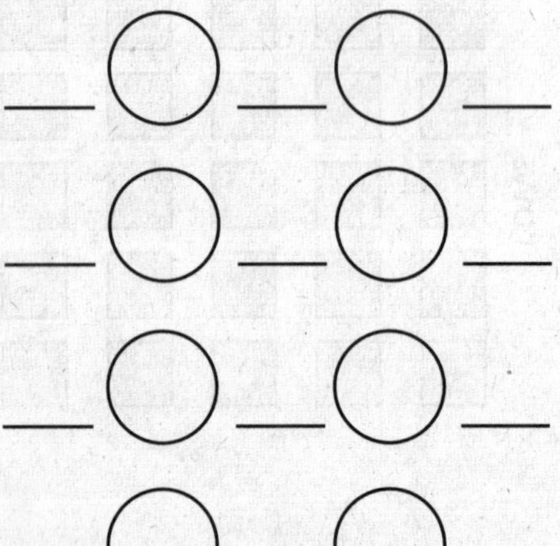

4. 4, 4, 16

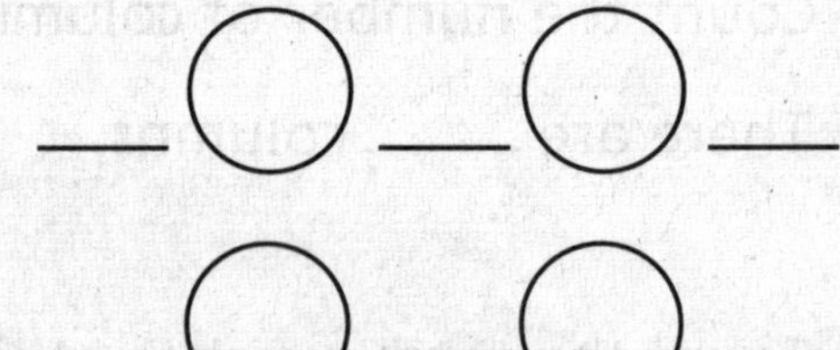

Check

5. Explain why you can write both multiplication and division sentences to describe an array.

____

____

____

____

____

____

Name____

Division Facts Through 5

Skill 41

Learn the Math

You can use different strategies to find the quotient.

Vocabulary

quotient

Divide. 24 ÷ 4

Draw a picture.

There are 6 groups of 4. So, 24 ÷ 4 = ___.

Count back on a number line.

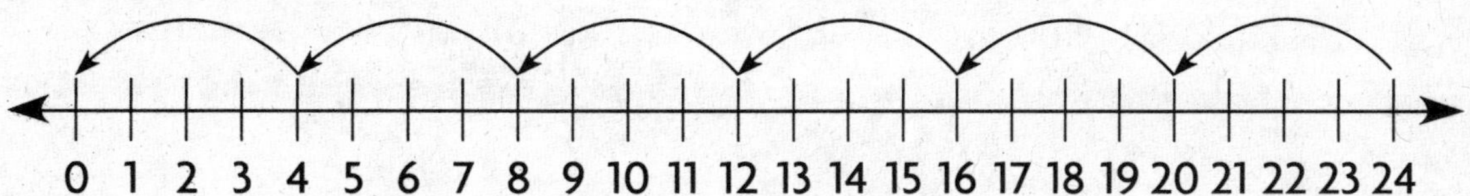

You subtract four 6 times. So, 24 ÷ 4 = ___.

Use an array.

Make an array with 24 tiles. Place 4 tiles in each row. Count the number of rows. There are 6 rows of four tiles.

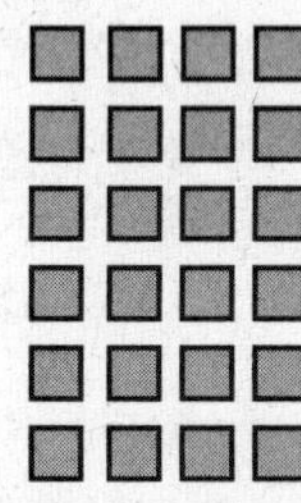

Since 6 × 4 = 24, then 24 ÷ 4 = ___.

Use a fact family.

Use a fact you know to find a fact you don't know.

Think: 4 × ___ = 24

So, 24 ÷ 4 = ___.

Do the Math

Choose a strategy. Find the quotient. Tell what strategy you used.

1. 12 ÷ 2 = _____

2. 25 ÷ 5 = _____

3. 16 ÷ 4 = _____

4. 32 ÷ 4 = _____

5. 15 ÷ 3 = _____

6. 40 ÷ 5 = _____

7. 18 ÷ 2 = _____

8. 21 ÷ 3 = _____

Check

9. Explain two different ways to find 20 ÷ 5.

____

____

____

____

Name ____________________

Part of a Whole

Skill 42

Learn the Math

A fraction can name part of a whole.

Vocabulary

equal parts
fraction

1 whole 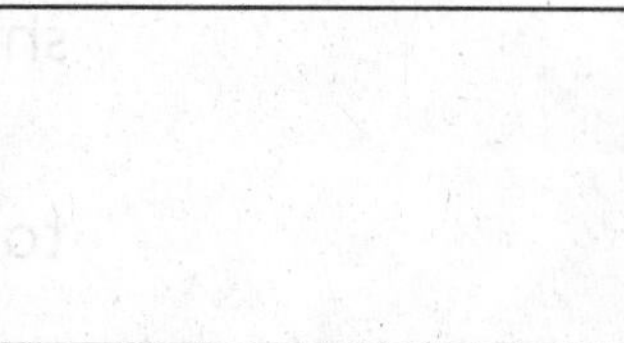

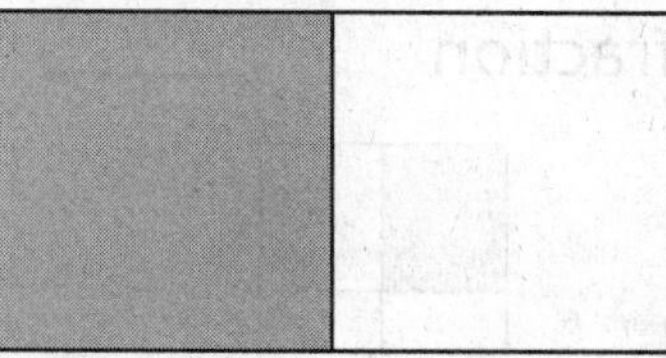

1 out of 2 equal parts is shaded.

$\frac{1}{2} = \frac{\text{1 shaded part}}{\text{2 equal parts}}$

2 out of 3 equal parts are shaded.

$\frac{2}{3} = \frac{\text{2 shaded parts}}{\text{3 equal parts}}$

What fraction of this figure is shaded?

Step 1

Count how many equal parts are in the whole. There are ____ equal parts.

1 2 3 ____

Step 2

Count how many equal parts are shaded. There are ____ shaded parts.

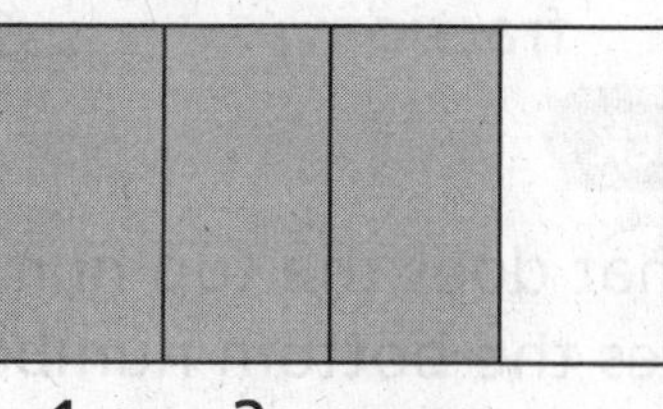

1 2 ____

Step 3

Write the fraction.

$\frac{3}{4}$ ← number of shaded parts / ← number of equal parts

____ out of ____ equal parts are shaded.

So, the fraction of the figure that is shaded is ____.

Do the Math

Skill 42

Write a fraction to name the shaded part.

1.

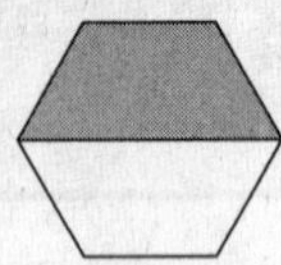

shaded parts ______

total parts ______

fraction ______

2.

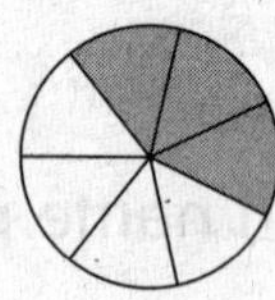

shaded parts ______

total parts ______

fraction ______

3.

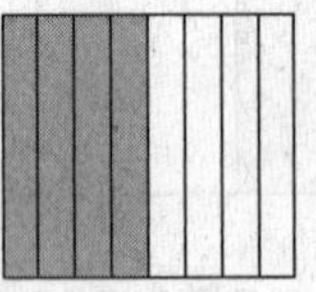

shaded parts ______

total parts ______

fraction ______

4.

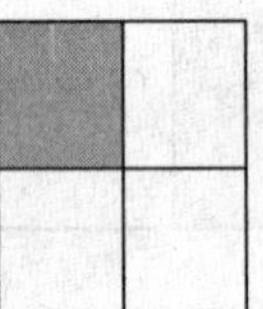

shaded parts ______

total parts ______

fraction ______

5.

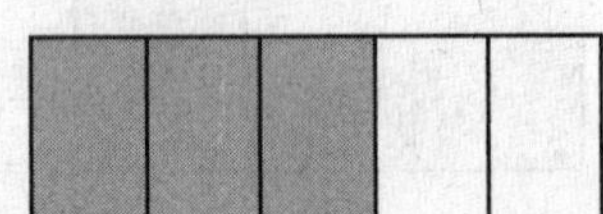

shaded parts ______

total parts ______

fraction ______

6.

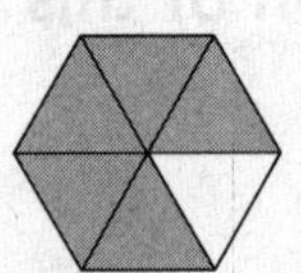

shaded parts ______

total parts ______

fraction ______

Check

7. What does the top number of a fraction tell you? What does the bottom number of a fraction tell you?

____

____

____

____

Name ____________________

Part of a Group
Skill 43

Learn the Math

A fraction can name part of a group.

Vocabulary

fraction

What fraction of the counters is shaded?

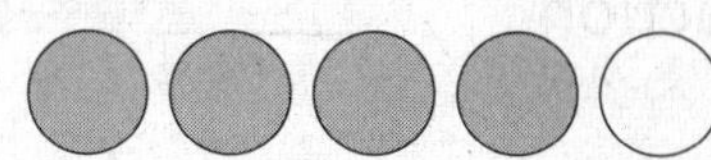

Step 1

Count how many counters are in the whole group.

There are ____ counters.

Step 2

Count how many counters are shaded.

There are ____ shaded counters.

Step 3

Write the fraction.

4 ← number of shaded counters
5 ← total number of counters

____ out of ____ counters are shaded.

So, the fraction of the group that is shaded is ____.

What fraction of the groups is shaded?

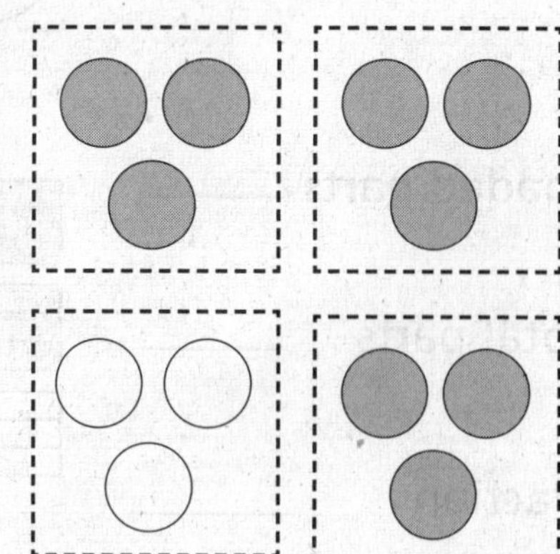

Step 1

Count the total number of groups.

There are ____ groups.

Step 2

Count how many groups are shaded.

There are ____ shaded groups.

Step 3

Write the fraction.

____ out of ____ groups are shaded.

So, the fraction of the groups that is shaded is ____.

Write a fraction that names the shaded part of the group.

1.
shaded parts ______
total parts ______
fraction ______

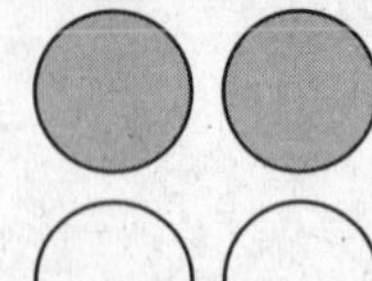

2.
shaded parts ______
total parts ______
fraction ______

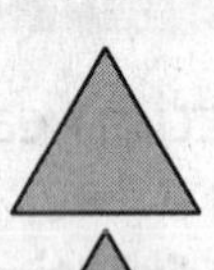
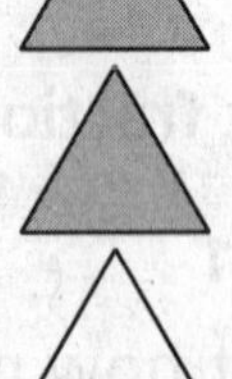

3.
shaded parts ______
total parts ______
fraction ______

4.
shaded parts ______
total parts ______
fraction ______

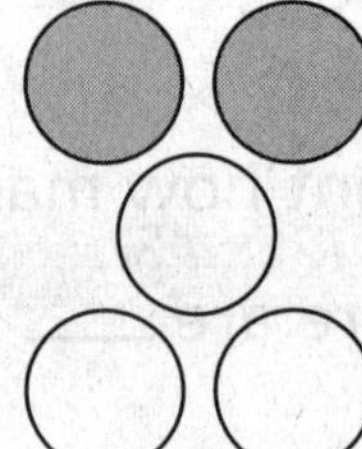

5.
shaded parts ______
total parts ______
fraction ______

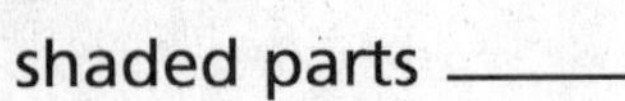
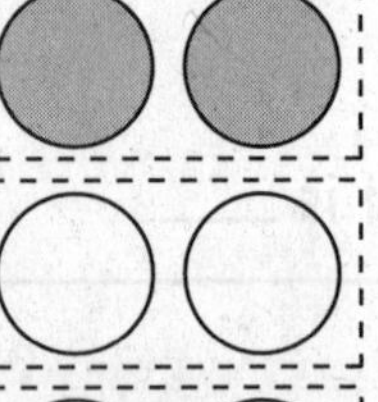
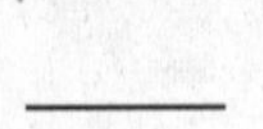

6.
shaded parts ______
total parts ______
fraction ______

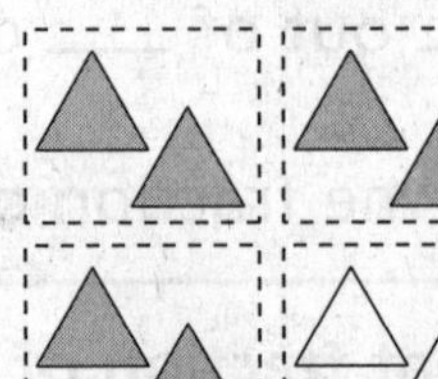
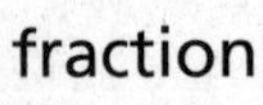
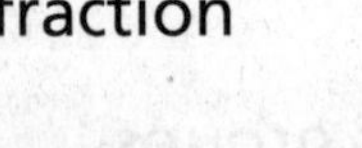

7.
shaded parts ______
total parts ______
fraction ______

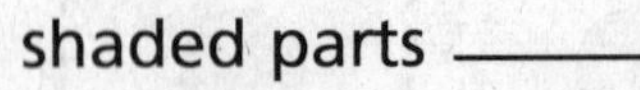
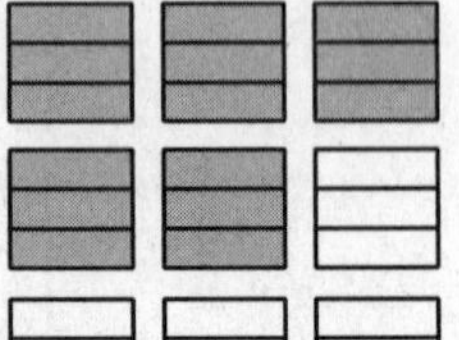
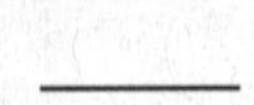

8.
shaded parts ______
total parts ______
fraction ______

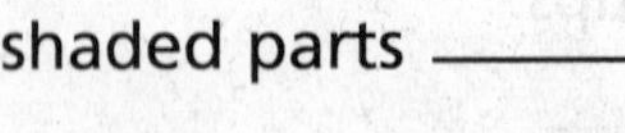

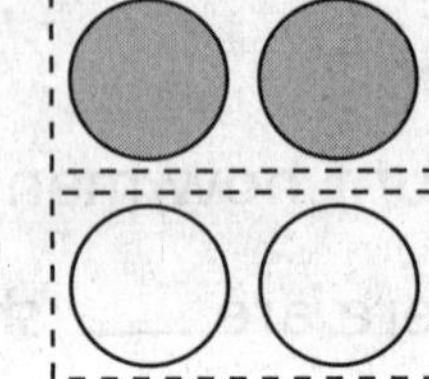

Check

9. What does the fraction $\frac{2}{8}$ mean?

____

____

Name____

Learn the Math

You can compare two fractions to see which is greater. Use <, >, or = to compare fractions.

Vocabulary

greater than (>)
less than (<)

Compare $\frac{1}{5}$ and $\frac{1}{2}$. Write <, >, or =.

Step 1

Make fraction strips to show $\frac{1}{5}$ and $\frac{1}{2}$.

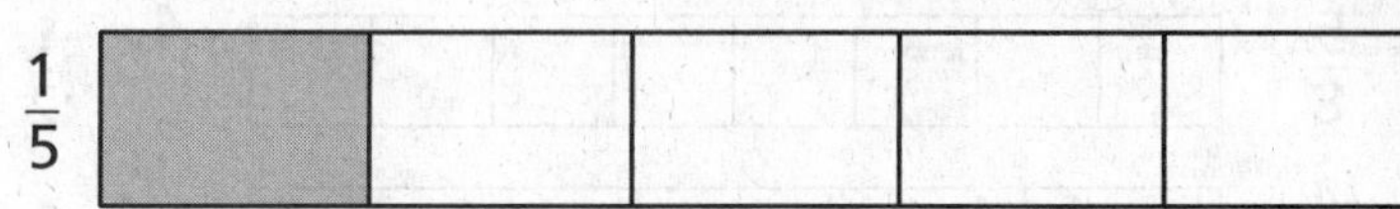

Step 2

Compare the fractions.
Which fraction strip has the greater length shaded? ____

So, $\frac{1}{5}$ ◯ $\frac{1}{2}$.

Compare $\frac{2}{4}$ and $\frac{1}{2}$. Write <, >, or =.

Step 1

Make fraction strips to show $\frac{2}{4}$ and $\frac{1}{2}$.

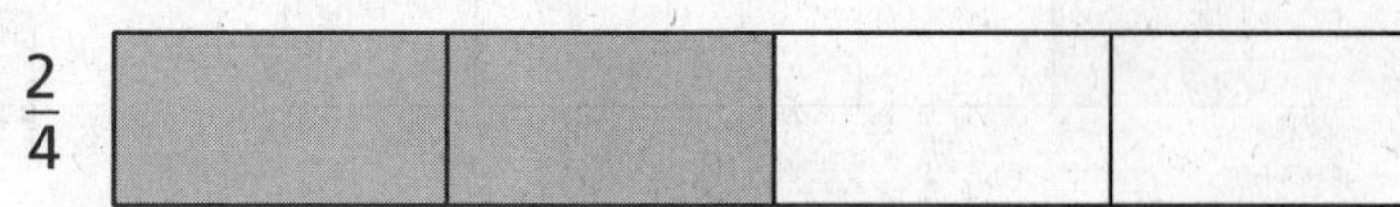

Step 2

Compare the fractions.
The fraction strips have the same length shaded.

So, $\frac{2}{4}$ ◯ $\frac{1}{2}$.

Do the Math

Color the fraction strips to show the fraction. Compare. Circle the greater fraction.

1. $\frac{5}{6}$ $\frac{4}{8}$

2. $\frac{2}{4}$ $\frac{2}{3}$

3. $\frac{5}{8}$ $\frac{4}{5}$

4. $\frac{1}{2}$ $\frac{1}{3}$

Compare the fractions. Write <, >, or =.

5.

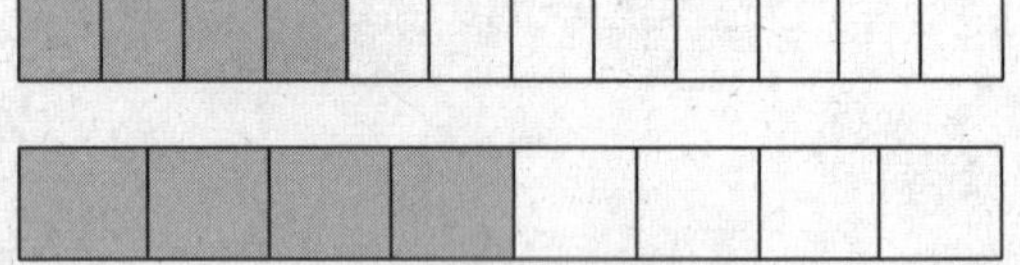

$\frac{4}{12}$ ◯ $\frac{4}{8}$

6.

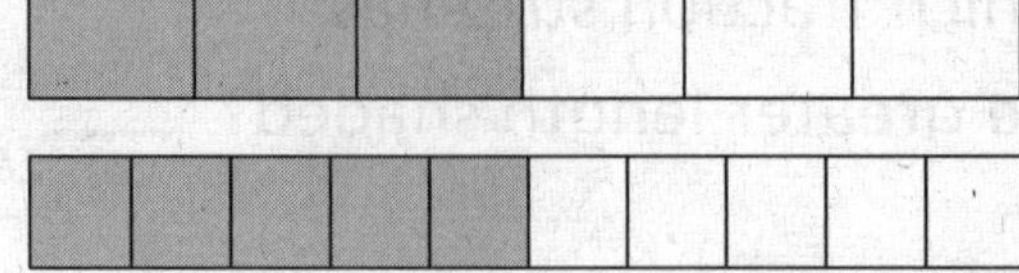

$\frac{3}{6}$ ◯ $\frac{5}{10}$

7.

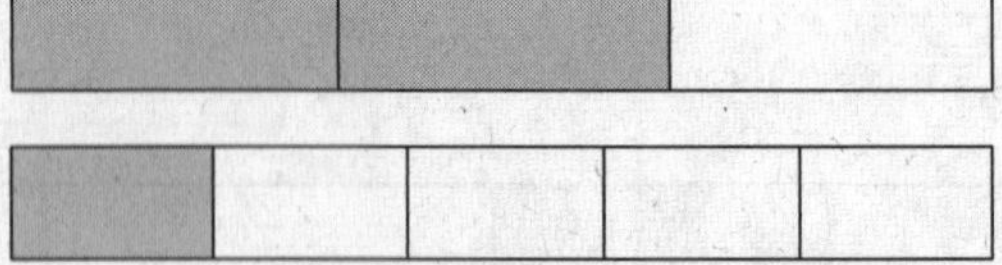

$\frac{2}{3}$ ◯ $\frac{1}{5}$

8.

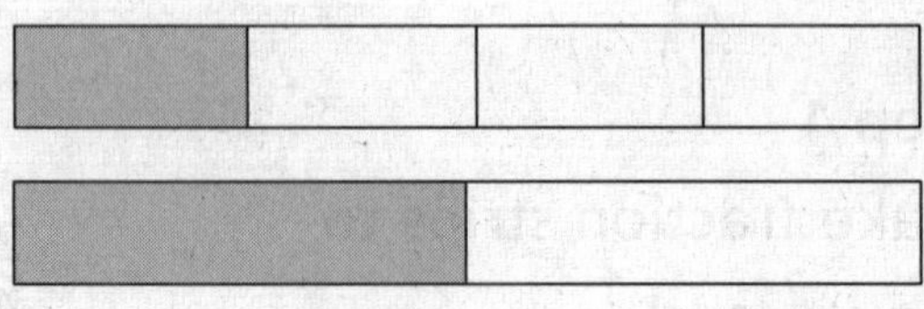

$\frac{1}{4}$ ◯ $\frac{1}{2}$

Check

9. How can you decide if one fraction is greater than another fraction?

____

____

____

____

Name ____________________

Fractions Equal to 1

Skill 45

Learn the Math

You can write a fraction for the whole.

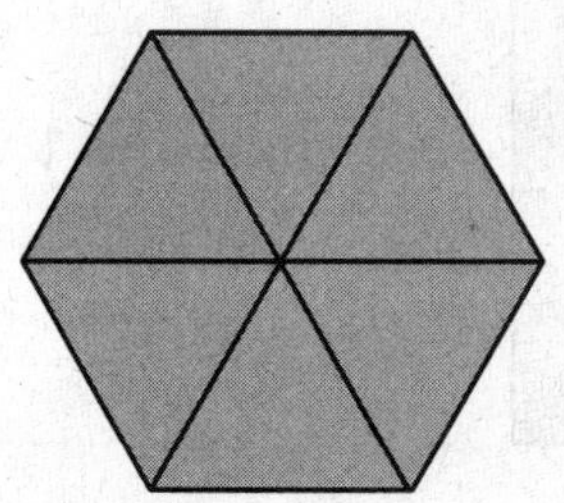

There are 6 shaded parts.

There are 6 equal parts.

Vocabulary

fraction

whole

$\frac{6}{6} = \frac{\text{6 shaded parts}}{\text{6 equal parts}}$

A fraction that names a whole is always equal to 1. $\frac{6}{6}$ = 1 whole

---

What fraction names this whole?

Think: The whole is divided into 4 equal parts.

Count all the fourths to make a whole.

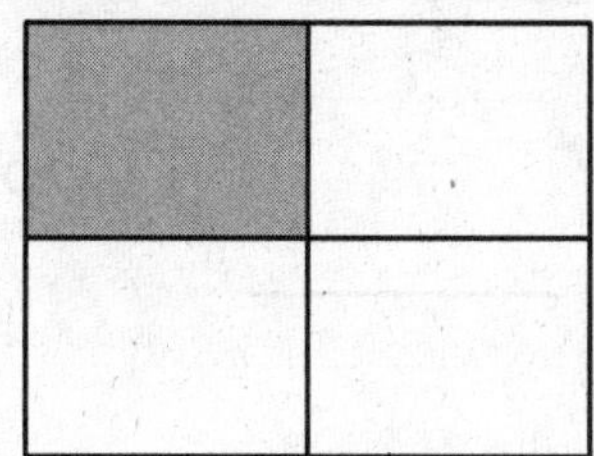

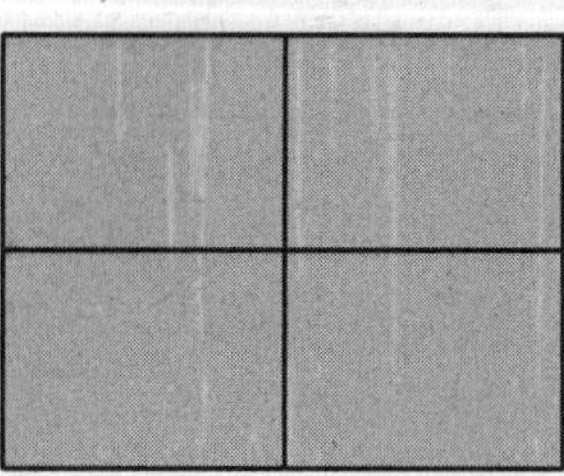

one fourth	two fourths	three fourths	four fourths
$\frac{1}{4}$	$\frac{2}{4}$	$\frac{3}{4}$	$\frac{4}{4}$

So, $\frac{\_\_}{4}$ names the whole. $\frac{\square}{4}$ = 1 whole

Write a fraction that names the whole.

1. 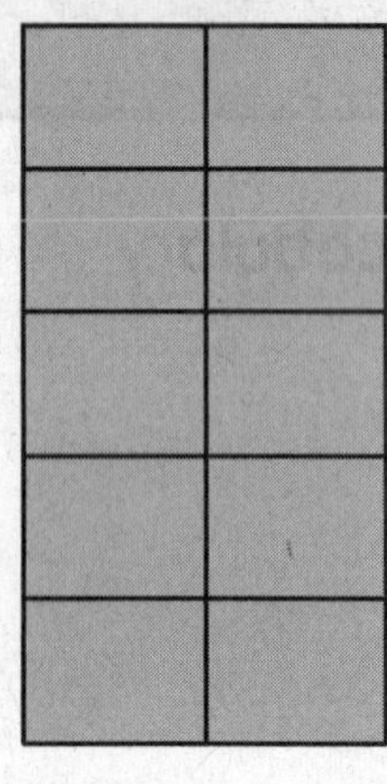

_____ = 1 whole

2. 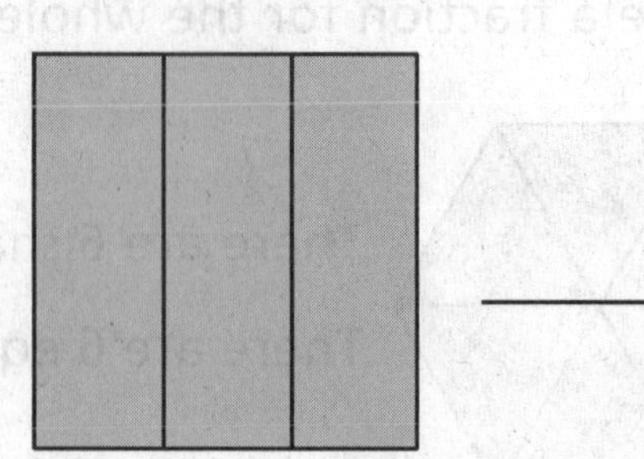

_____ = 1 whole

3. 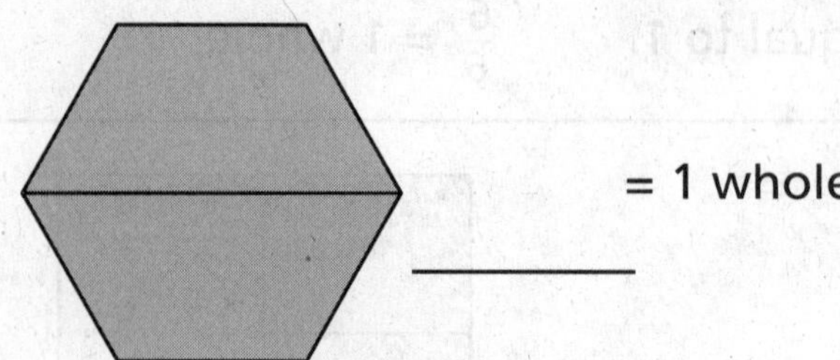

_____ = 1 whole

4. 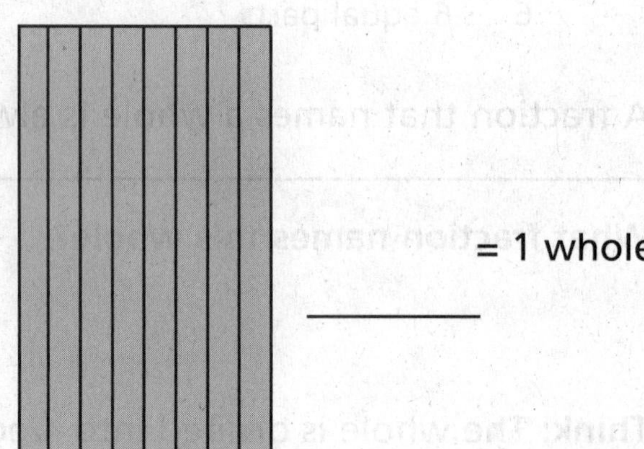

_____ = 1 whole

5. 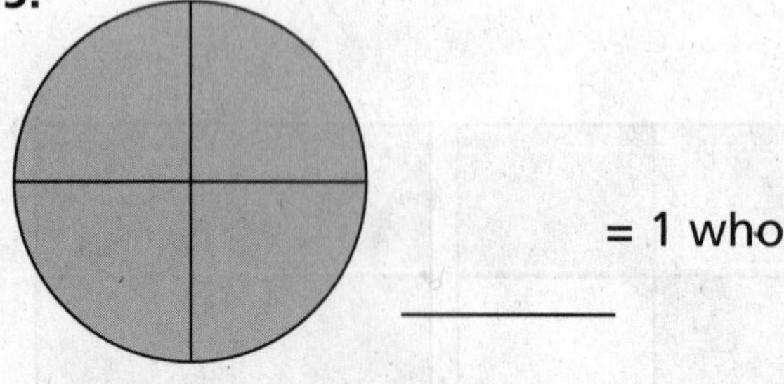

_____ = 1 whole

6. 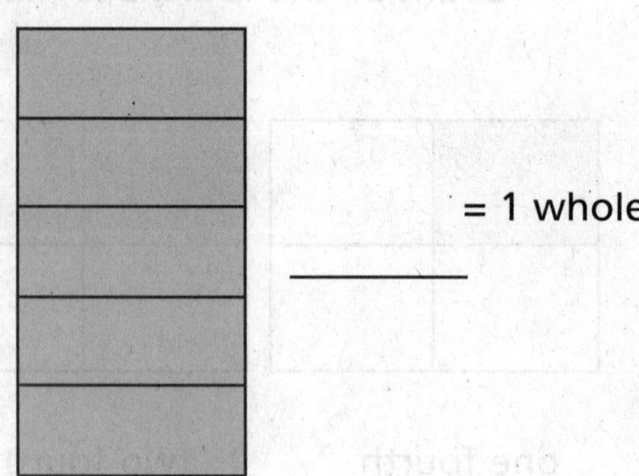

_____ = 1 whole

Check

7. If a circle is divided into eighths, what fraction names the whole? How do you know? What whole number is the fraction equal to?

____

____

____

____

Name ______________________________

Count Coins

Skill 46

Learn the Math

quarter	dime	nickel	penny
25¢	10¢	5¢	1¢

Vocabulary

quarter
dime
nickel
penny

You can count coins to find the total value. Start with the coins of greatest value. Count on to find the total.

Start at 25.

Count by 25s.	Count by tens.	Count by fives.	Count by ones.
25¢, 50¢,	60¢, 70¢,	75¢, 80¢,	81¢, 82¢

So, the total value of the coins is _____ .

Find the total value.

__25__ ¢, __35__ ¢, _____ ¢, _____ ¢, _____ ¢, _____ ¢

So, the total value of the coins is _____ .

Do the Math

Skill 46

Find the total value.

1.    

_____ ¢, _____ ¢, _____ ¢, _____ ¢, _____ ¢ total value

2.      

_____ ¢, _____ ¢, _____ ¢, _____ ¢, _____ ¢, _____ ¢ total value

3.     

_____ ¢, _____ ¢, _____ ¢, _____ ¢, _____ ¢ total value

4.      

_____ ¢, _____ ¢, _____ ¢, _____ ¢, _____ ¢, _____ ¢ total value

Check

5. Look back at Problem 3. What is the value of the quarters? What is the value of the nickels?

Value of quarters: _____ Value of nickels: _____

Name______________________________

One Dollar
Skill 47

Learn the Math

100 cents is the same as one dollar.

100¢ = $1.00

dollar sign (points to $) — decimal point (points to .)

1 penny = $0.01

100 pennies = $1.00

Vocabulary

dollar

1 nickel = $0.05

20 nickels = $1.00

1 dime = $0.10

10 dimes = $1.00

1 quarter = $0.25

4 quarters = $1.00

1 half dollar = $0.50

2 half dollars = $1.00

Circle coins to make one dollar.

Circle coins to make one dollar.

1.

2.

3.

Check

4. Look back at Problem 1. List another group of coins you could circle to make one dollar.

____

____

Name ____________________

Learn the Math

You can count a dollar bill and coins to find the total value. Start with the dollar bill. Then count on. Order the coins from greatest value to least value.

Start at $1.00.	Count on 25.	Count by tens.	Count by fives.	Count by ones.
$1.00	$1.25	$1.35	$1.40	$1.41

The total value is $ ______.

Find the total value.

$1.00, **$1.10**, ______, ______, ______

The total value is $ ______.

______, ______, ______, ______, ______

The total value is ______.

Find the total value.

1.

________, ________, ________, ________

____

2.

________, ________, ________, ________, ________

____

3.

________, ________, ________, ________, ________

____

Check

4. Look back at Problem 2. Show another way to find the same amount, using one dollar and cents.

____

____

Name________________________________

Time to the Hour

Skill 49

Learn the Math

A clock measures time in hours and minutes.
There are 60 minutes in one hour.

Vocabulary

hour
hour hand
minute hand
minute

The clocks below show time to the hour.

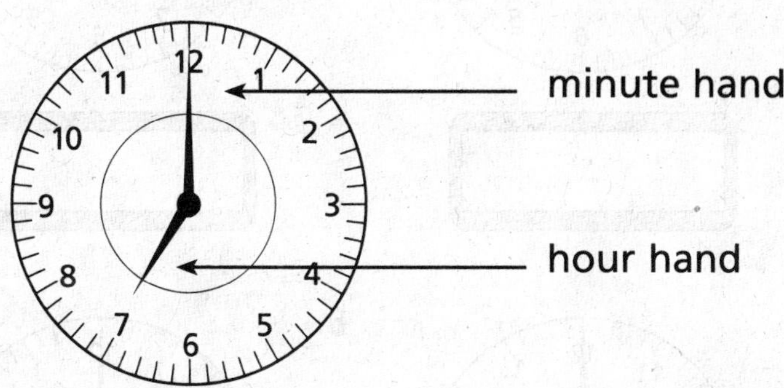

The minute hand points to 12.

The hour hand points to 10.

The time on these clocks is ________ .

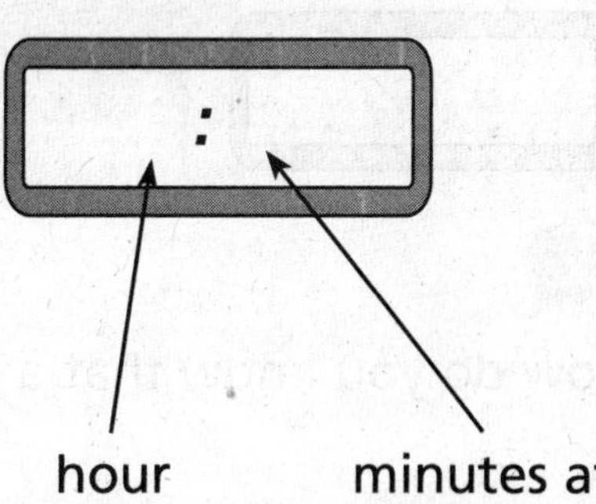

The minute hand points to ________.

The hour hand points to ________.

The time on these clocks is ________ .

Do the Math

Skill 49

Write the time.

1.

:

2.

:

3.

:

4.

:

5.

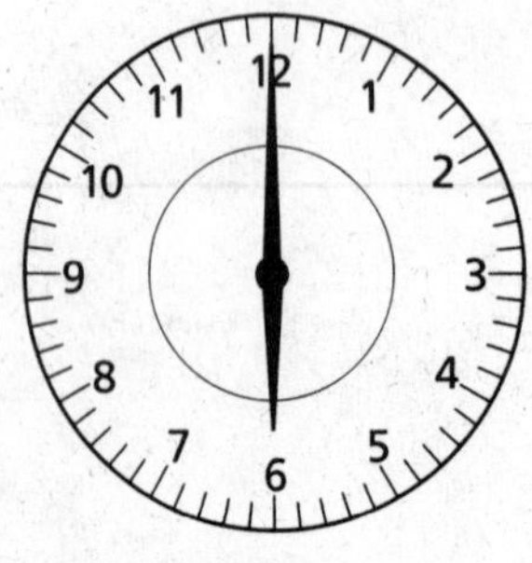

:

6.

:

7.

:

8.

:

9.

:

Check

10. How do you know that a clock is showing time exactly on the hour?

Name____________________

Time to the Half Hour

Skill 50

Learn the Math

There are 30 minutes in a half hour. You can read and write times to the half hour.

Vocabulary

half hour

What time does this clock show?

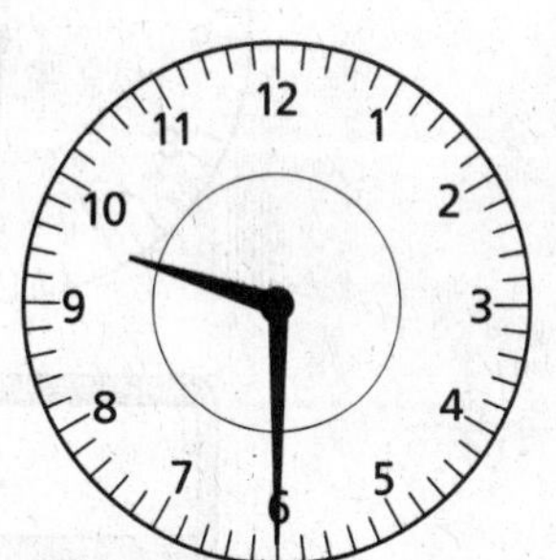

Step 1

Look at the hour hand. The hour hand points halfway between 9 and 10. This means the hour is 9.

Step 2

Look at the minute hand. The minute hand points to 6. This means it is 30 minutes after the hour.

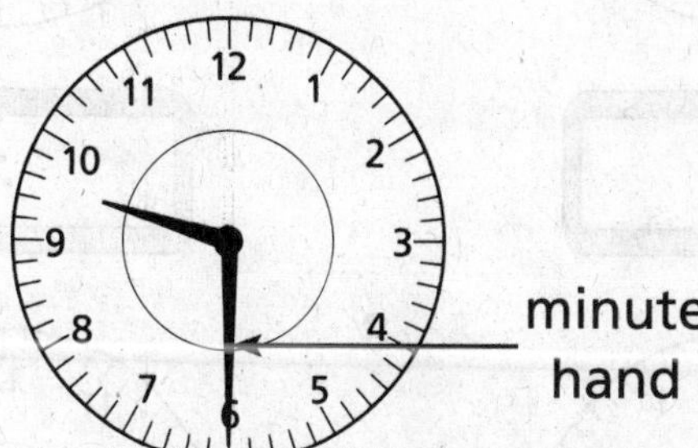

So, the clock shows 9:30.

What time does this clock show?

Step 1

Look at the hour. The number on the left shows the hour.

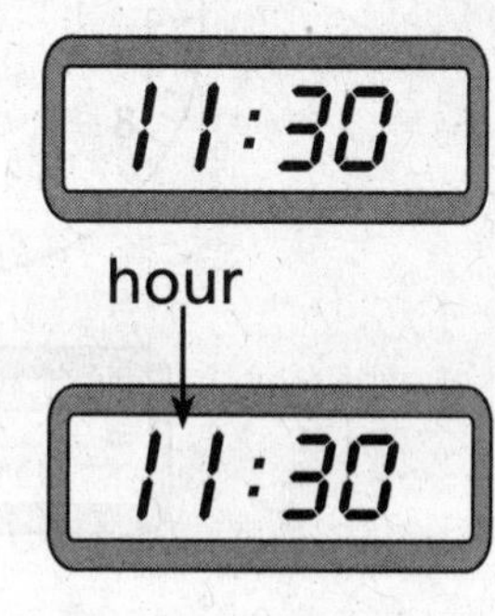

Step 2

Look at the minutes. The number on the right shows the minutes after the hour.

It is _____ minutes after _____.

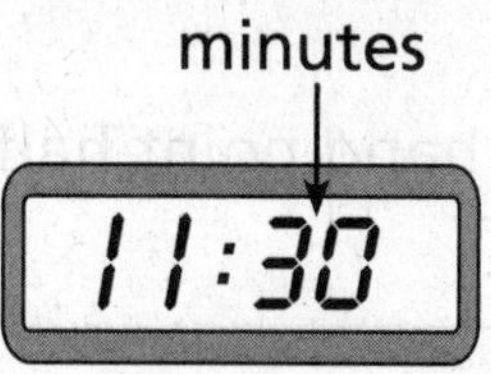

So, the clock shows 11:30.

Write the time.

1. 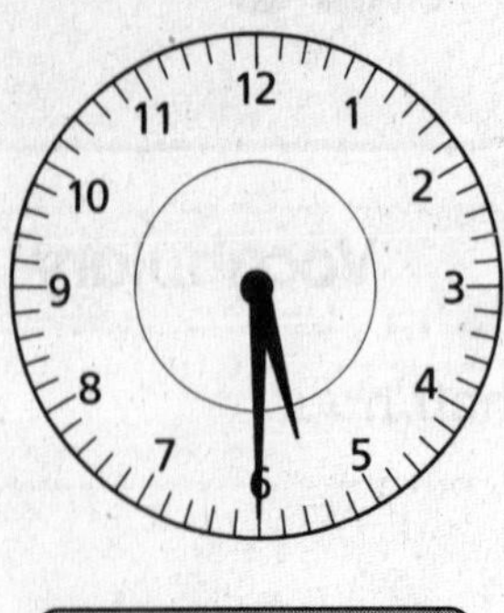

:

2. 

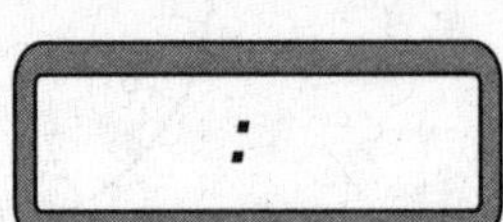
:

3. 

:

4. 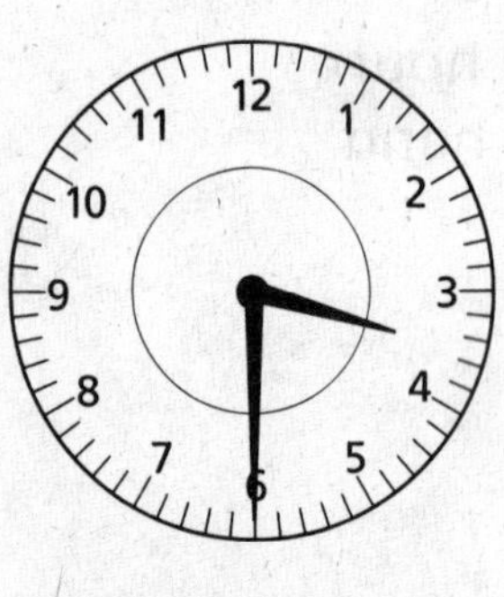

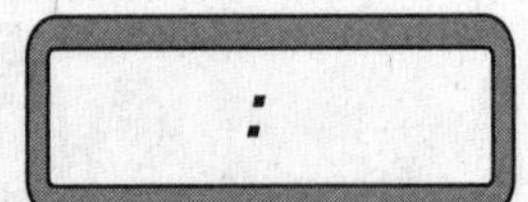
:

5. 

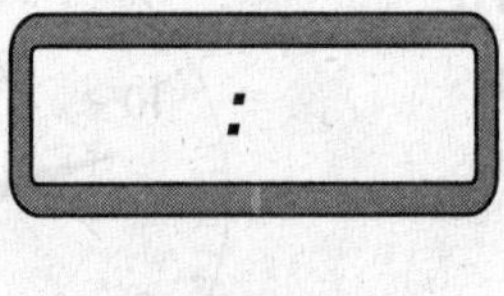
:

6. 

:

7.

:

8.

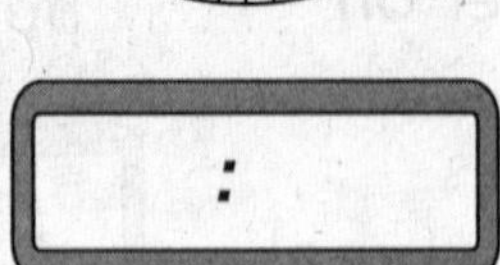
:

9. 

:

Check

10. Why does the hour hand point halfway between 8 and 9 at 8:30?

____

____

Name____________________

Time to the Quarter Hour

Skill 51

Learn the Math

Vocabulary

quarter hour

A quarter hour is 15 minutes. You can read and write time to the quarter hour.

What time does this clock show?

Step 1

Look at the hour hand.

The hour hand points between 2 and 3.

This means the hour is 2.

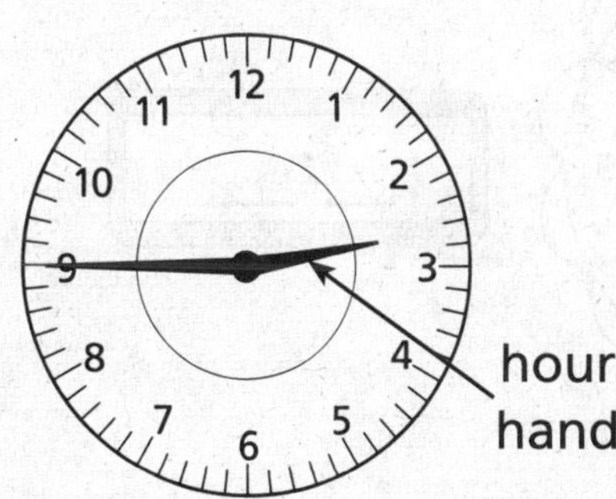

Step 2

Look at the minute hand.
The minute hand points to 9.

It takes 5 minutes for the minute hand to move from one number to the next. Count by fives 9 times to find the number of minutes.

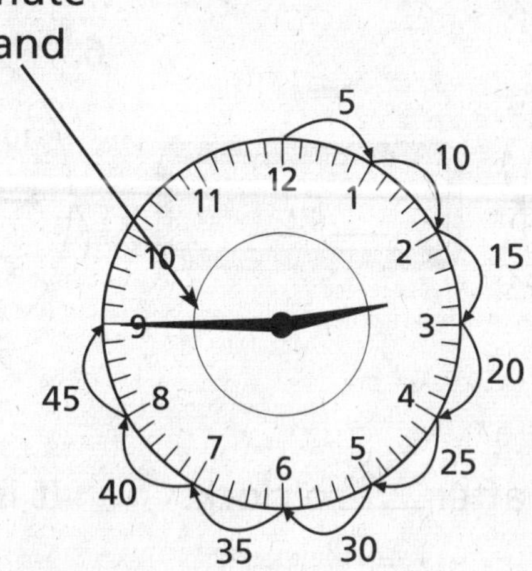

Say: 5, 10, 15, 20, 25, 30, 35, 40, 45.

It is ____ minutes after the hour.

So, it is ____ minutes after 2 o'clock or 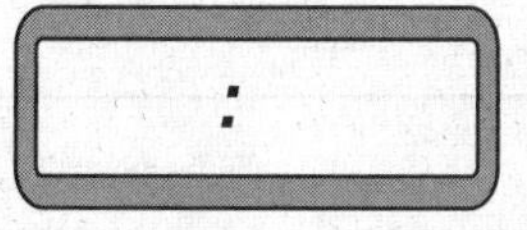 .

Write the time in two ways.

1.

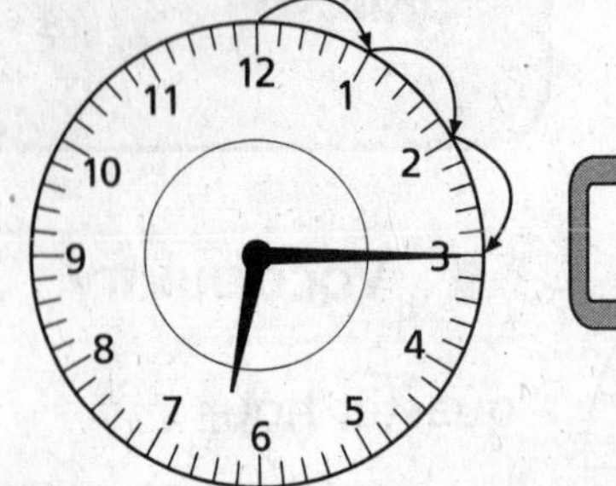

___ : ___

It is ____ minutes after ____ o'clock.

2.

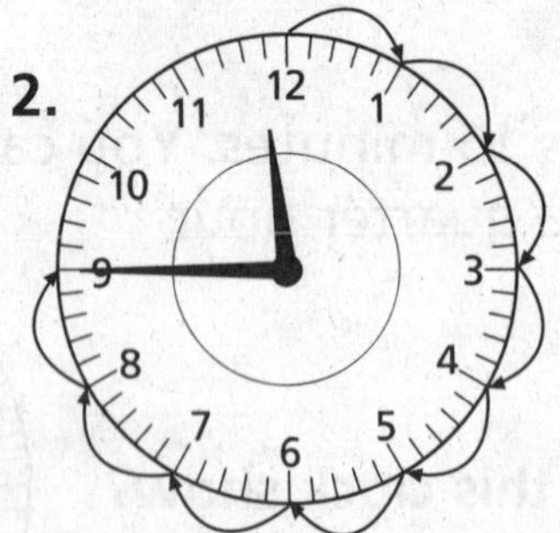

___ : ___

It is ____ minutes after ____ o'clock.

3.

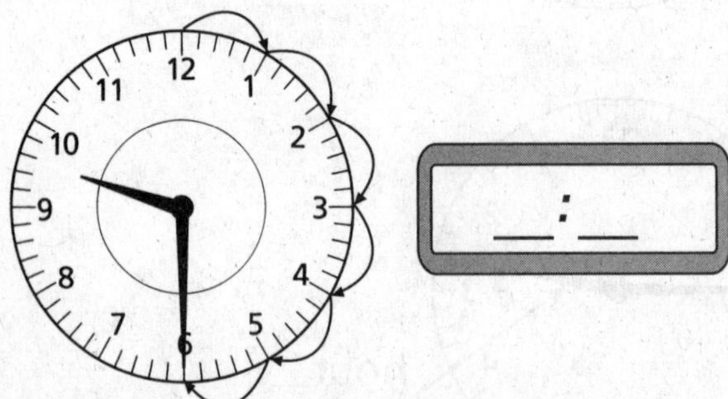

It is ____ minutes after ____ o'clock.

4.

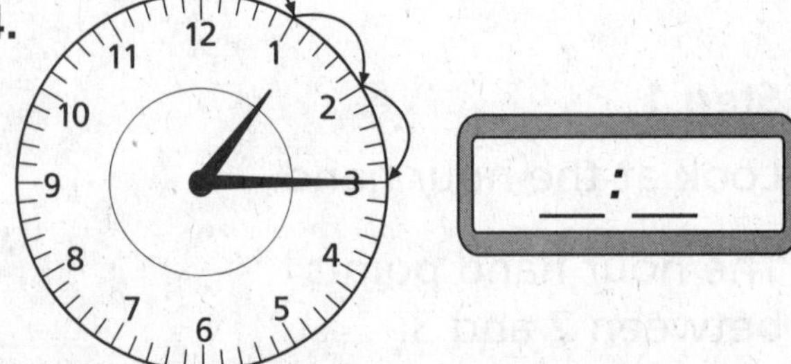

It is ____ minutes after ____ o'clock.

5.

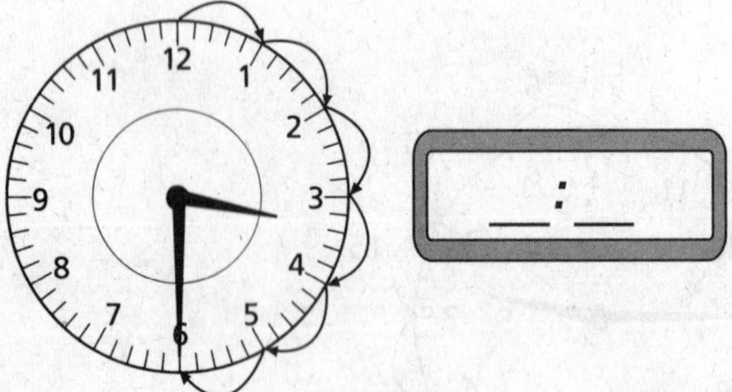

It is ____ minutes after ____ o'clock.

6.

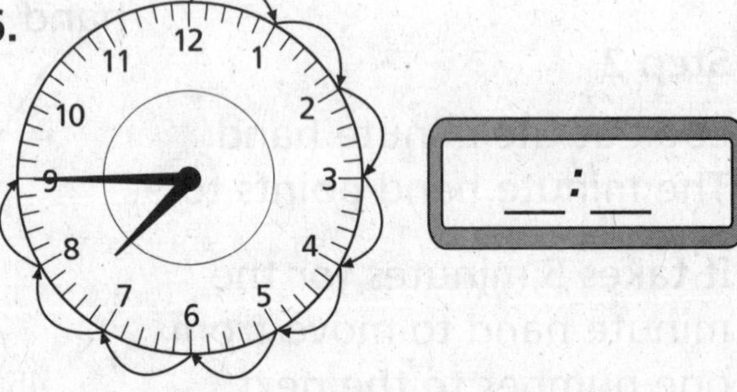

It is ____ minutes after ____ o'clock.

Check

7. What time is it when the hour hand is between the 4 and 5 and the minute hand is on the 9? How do you know?

____

____

____

____

Name____

Read a Thermometer

Skill 52

Learn the Math

A thermometer is used to measure temperature. Temperature can be measured in degrees Fahrenheit (°F).

Vocabulary

degrees Fahrenheit (°F)
temperature
thermometer

What temperature does this thermometer show?

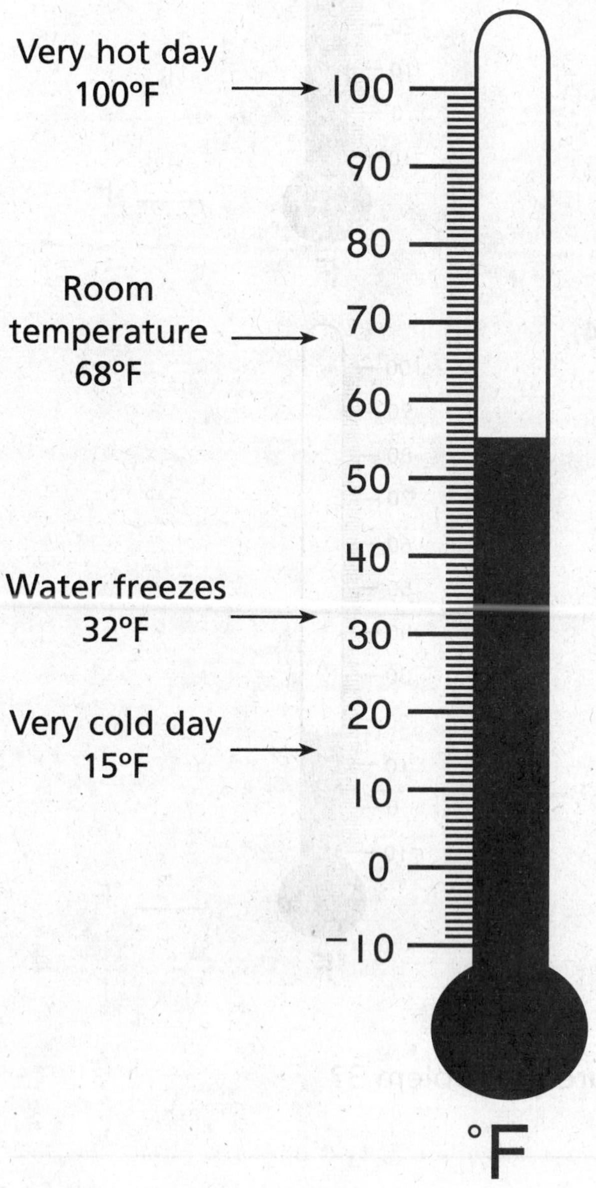

Very hot day 100°F → 100
90
80
Room temperature 68°F → 70
60
50
Water freezes 32°F → 40
30
Very cold day 15°F → 20
10
0
−10
°F

Step 1
The black bar in the center of the thermometer rises and falls with the temperature.

Step 2
To read the thermometer, find the line on the scale closest to the top of the black bar. Then use the scale to identify the number that the line stands for.

On this thermometer, the top of the black bar is between _____ °F and _____ °F.

Think: Each line stands for 1 degree. Count on from 50. Count by ones.

So, the thermometer shows a temperature of _____ °F.

Say: fifty-five degrees Fahrenheit

Write: ________

Write each temperature.

1.

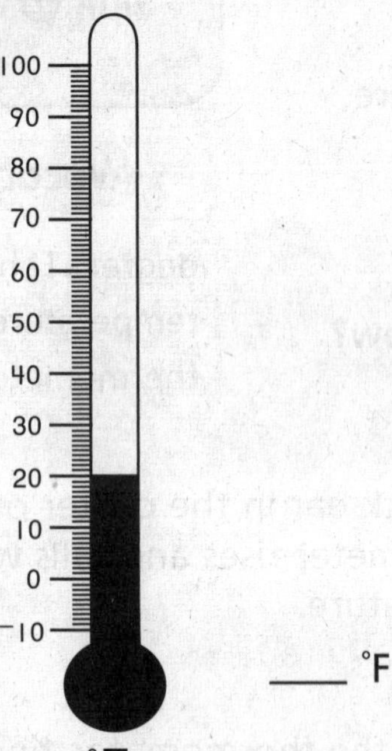

____ °F

2.

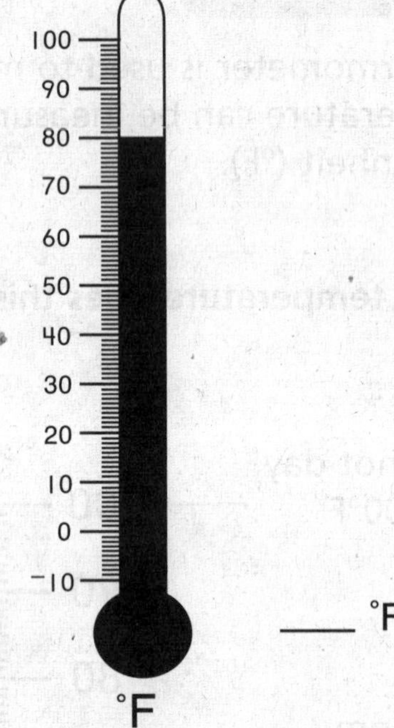

____ °F

3.

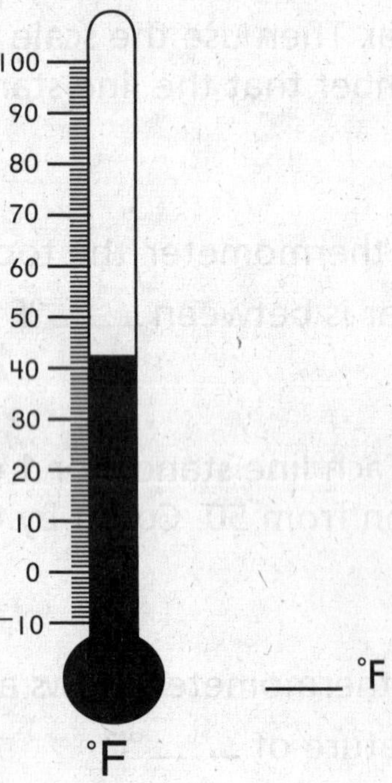

____ °F

4.

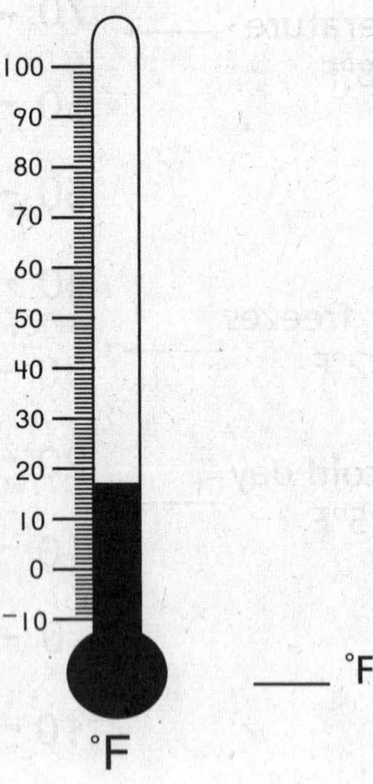

____ °F

Check

5. Explain how you found the temperature in Problem 3?

____

____

____

Name______________________________

Read Tables and Charts

Skill 53

Learn the Math

Tables and charts display data. You can read a table or chart to answer questions.

This table shows how many different kinds of plants are in a class garden.

Plants in Class Garden	
Type of Plant	**Number**
Flower	5
Herb	4
Vegetable	3

How many herb plants are in the garden?

Think: Find the row with the word *herb*.
Look to the right to find how many.

There are___ herb plants in the garden.

This chart shows the weather each day for one week.

Weather This Week						
Sunday	Monday	Tuesday	Wednesday	Thursday	Friday	Saturday
sunny	sunny	cloudy	rainy	sunny	cloudy	sunny

Were there more sunny days or more cloudy days?

Think: How many sunny days were there? ___
How many cloudy days were there? ___
Compare. 4 ___ 2

There were more ________ days.

Vocabulary

chart
data
table

Do the Math

Use the table at the right to answer the questions.

Rainfall	
Month	**Amount of Rain**
June	7 centimeters
July	6 centimeters
August	3 centimeters
September	11 centimeters

1. How much rain fell in June?

____ centimeters

2. Which month had the most rainfall?

____

3. How much more rain fell in July than in August?

____ centimeters

Use the chart below to answer the questions.

Places We Saw Insects				
Garden	Barn	Field	Pond	Park
Ladybug	Butterfly	Butterfly	Dragonfly	Butterfly

4. Which insect was seen most often? ________________

5. Where were ladybugs seen? ________________

6. In how many places were insects seen? ____ places

Check

7. Use the table at the top of the page. List the months in order from the least amount of rain to the greatest amount of rain.

____

____

____

____

Name ___

Read a Tally Table

Skill 54

Learn the Math

Information collected about people or things is called data.

A tally table uses tally marks to show data.

This tally table shows the favorite flowers of sixteen students.

Vocabulary

data

tally mark

tally table

Our Favorite Flowers	
Flower	**Tally**
daisy	~~IIII~~
marigold	IIII
pansy	~~IIII~~ II

On a tally table, each tally mark stands for 1.

This is one tally mark. I   This is five tally marks. ~~IIII~~

How many students chose pansy as their favorite flower?

Step 1

Look at the table.

Find the row for pansy.

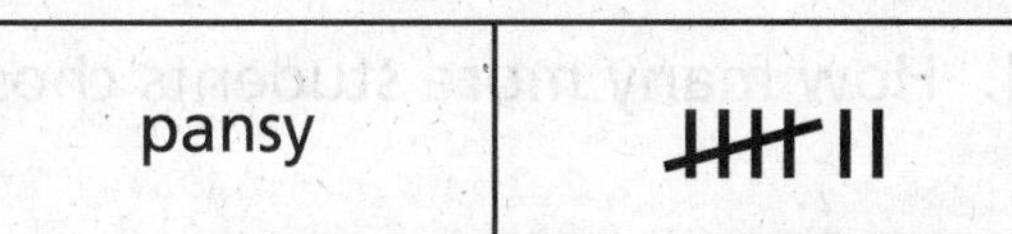

Step 2

Count the tally marks in that row.

Think: Start with ___. Count on by 1s.

5, ___, ___

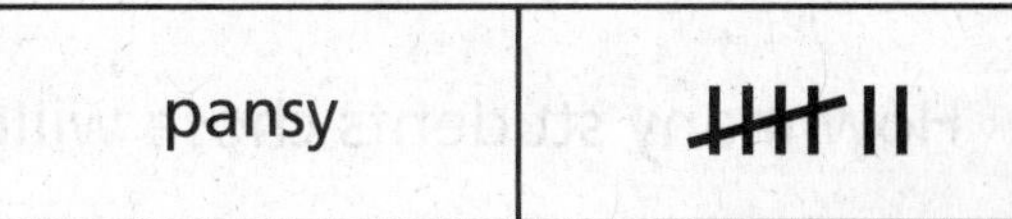

Step 3

The number of tally marks shows the number of students that chose pansy.

Think: There are ___ tally marks in the row for pansy.

So, ___ students chose pansy as their favorite flower.

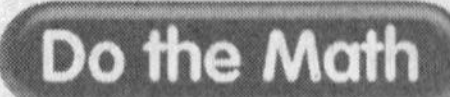

Use the tally table to answer the questions.

Our Favorite Trees	
Tree	**Tally**
oak	IIII
pine	III
cherry	~~IIII~~ III
maple	II
willow	~~IIII~~ I

1. How many students chose oak? ____ students

2. How many students chose willow? ____ students

3. Did more students choose maple or pine? ____________

4. How many more students chose cherry than chose pine? ____ more students

5. Which tree was the favorite of the most students? ____________

6. How many students chose willow or oak? ____ students

Check

7. Use the table at the top of the page. How many students voted in all? Explain how you know.

____

____

____

____

Name ____________________

Read a Bar Graph
Skill 55

Learn the Math

A bar graph uses bars to show information.

This bar graph tells how some students get to school.

Vocabulary

bar graph

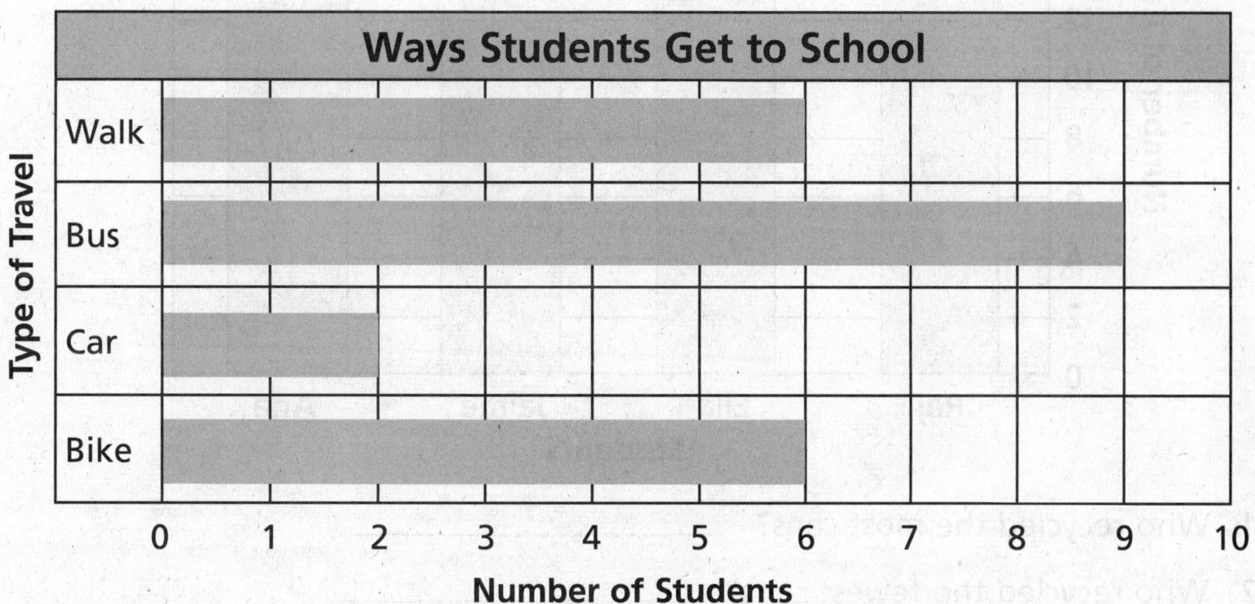

The length of each bar is equal to the number of students that travel to school in that way. Look at where each bar ends. This tells how many.

How many students ride a bus to school?

Find the row labeled bus. Look at where the bar ends. The number tells you how many.

So, ____ students ride a bus to school.

How many more students travel to school by bike than by car?

Think: How many students travel to school by bike? ____

How many students travel to school by car? ____

Subtract to find how many more students travel by bike. 6 – 2 = ____

So, ____ more students travel to school by bike than by car.

Use the bar graph to answer the questions.

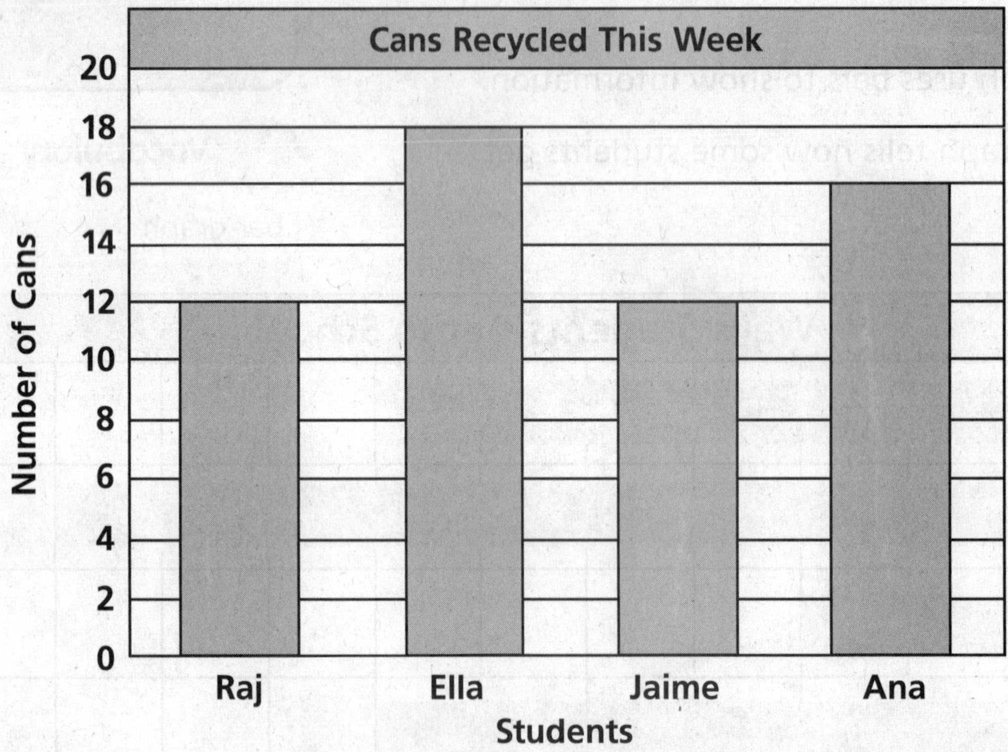

1. Who recycled the most cans? ________________
2. Who recycled the fewest cans? ________________
3. How many cans did Ana recycle? ____ cans
4. How many cans did Raj recycle? ____ cans
5. How many more cans did Ana recycle than Raj? ____ cans
6. How many cans did Raj and Ella recycle in all? ____ cans

Check

7. Explain how you answered Problem 6.

____

____

____

____

____

____

Name ______________________________

Make a List

Skill 56

Learn the Math

Vocabulary

combination

list

You can make a list to help you organize information and count possible combinations.

How many different combinations of ice cream and toppings are there?

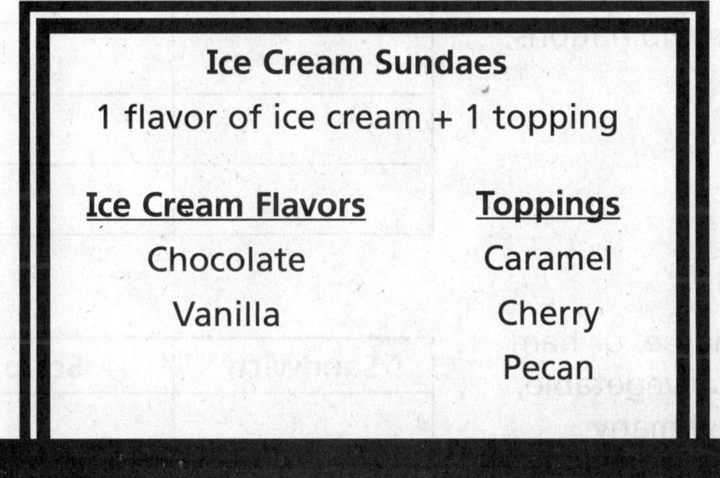

Make a list to show the possible sundae combinations. List each ice cream flavor with each topping.

	Ice Cream	Topping
1.	Chocolate	Caramel
2.	Chocolate	Cherry
3.	Chocolate	Pecan
4.		
5.		
6.		

The list shows how many different sundae combinations there are.

There are ____ possible combinations.

Do the Math

Make a list to show the possible combinations.
Then tell how many combinations are possible.

1. Chloe has a green shirt, a blue shirt, and a white shirt. She has tan pants and black pants. How many combinations of 1 shirt and 1 pair of pants are possible?

Shirt	Pants

There are ____ possible combinations.

2. Jose can buy a turkey, cheese, or ham sandwich. He can also buy vegetable, tomato, or pea soup. How many combinations of 1 soup and 1 sandwich are possible?

Sandwich	Soup

There are ____ possible combinations.

Check

3. Look back at Problem 1. How would the list change if Chloe also had a red shirt?

____

____

____

____

Name____

Outcomes

Skill 57

Learn the Math

When you toss a coin, there are two possible results. A possible result is called an outcome.

Vocabulary

outcome

What are the possible outcomes for tossing a coin?

Look at the coin.

heads up

tails up

Think: If you toss the coin, what might be the result?

The coin could land ________ up.

The coin could land ________ up.

So, the possible outcomes are ________ and ________.

What are the possible outcomes for this spinner?

Look at the spinner.

Think: If you spin the pointer, what might be the result?

The pointer could land on ________.

The pointer could land on ________.

The pointer could land on ________.

So, the possible outcomes are ________, ________, and ________.

List the possible outcomes.

1. Jeff will toss a cube numbered 1–6.

____

2. Jill will use this spinner.

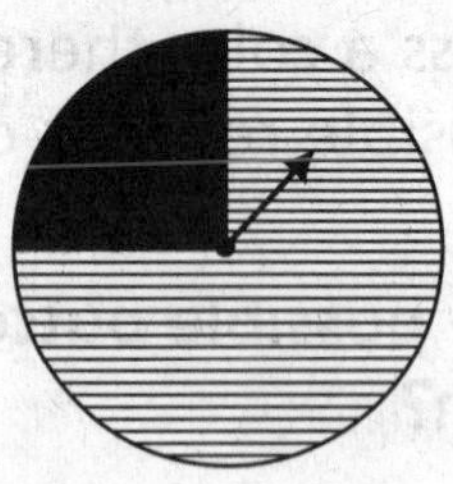

____

3. Gina will use this spinner.

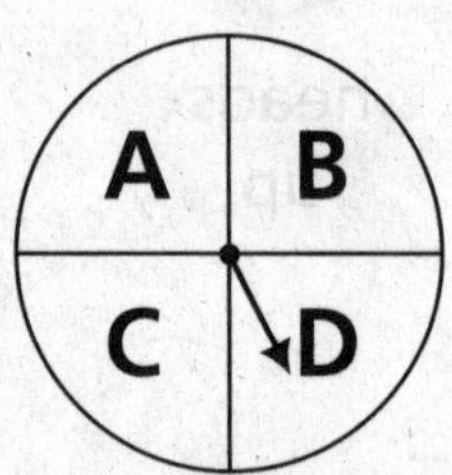

____

4. Max will draw 1 card from this box.

____

5. Nick will use this spinner.

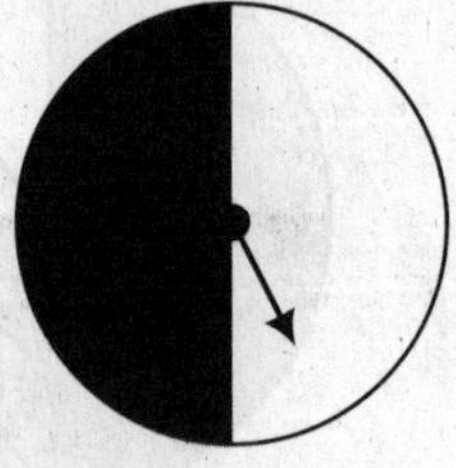

____

6. Liz will use this spinner.

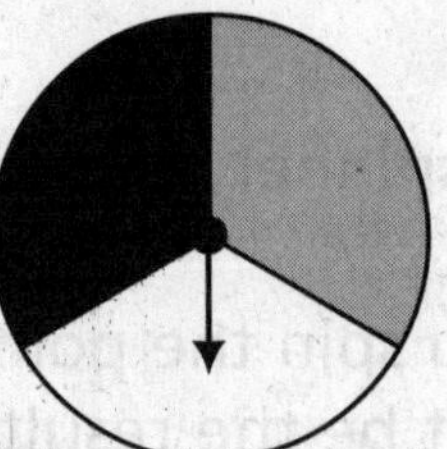

____

Check

7. Look at the spinner in Problem 5. Explain why gray cannot be an outcome.

____

____

____

Name ____________________

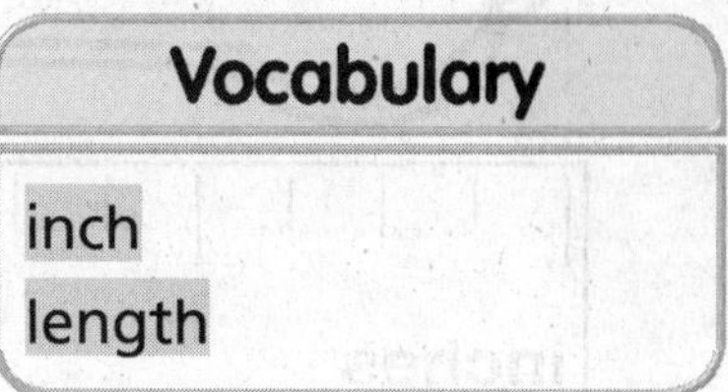

Learn the Math

You can use an inch ruler to measure the length of an object.

Vocabulary

inch
length

About how long is the spoon?

Step 1 Line up the left end of the spoon with the 0 mark on the ruler.

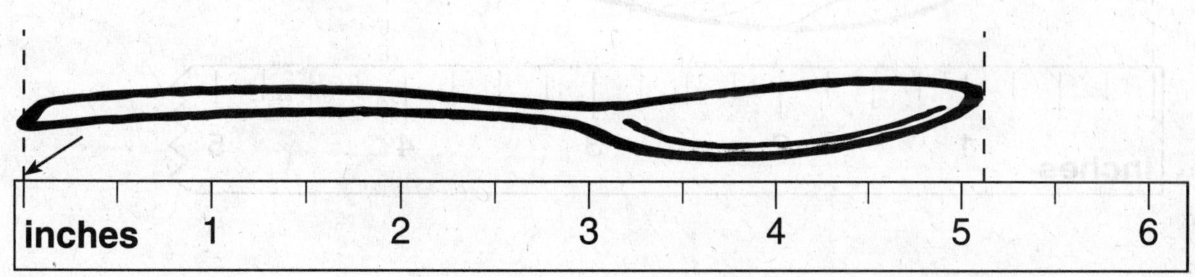

Step 2 Find the number that is closest to the right end of the spoon.

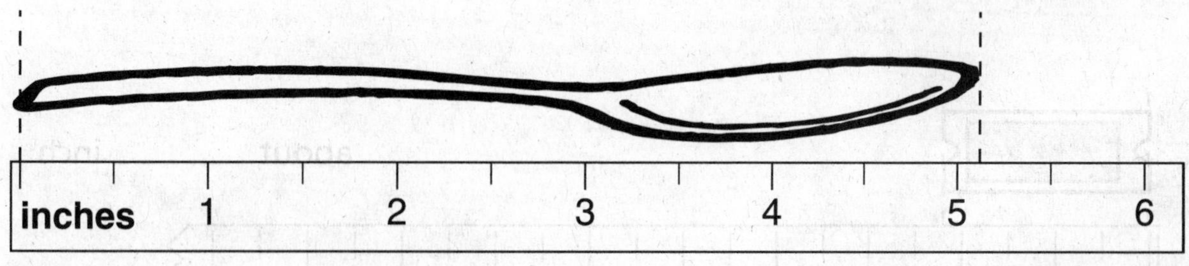

What number lines up closest to the right end of the spoon? ____

So, the spoon is about ____ inches long.

Use an inch ruler to measure. Find the length in inches.

1.

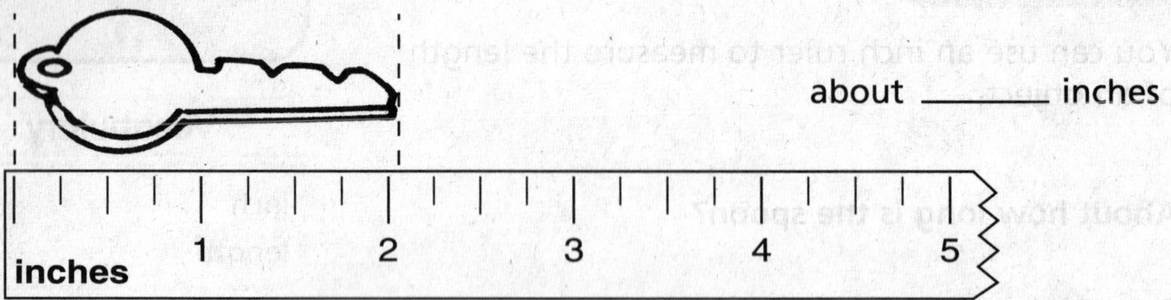

about ______ inches

2.

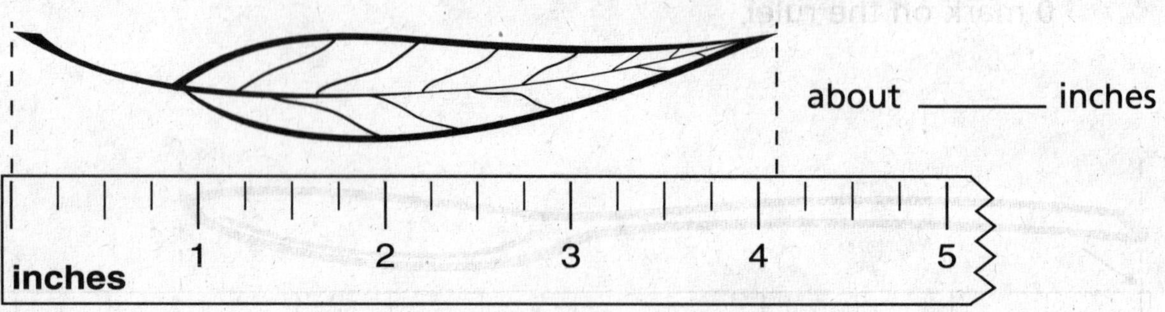

about ______ inches

3.

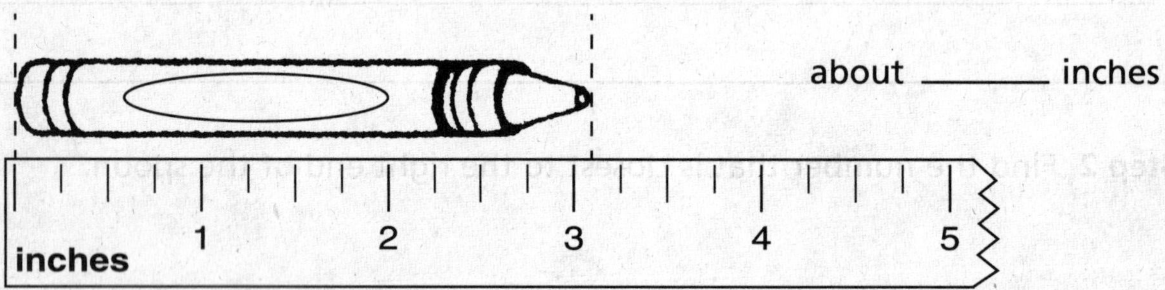

about ______ inches

4.

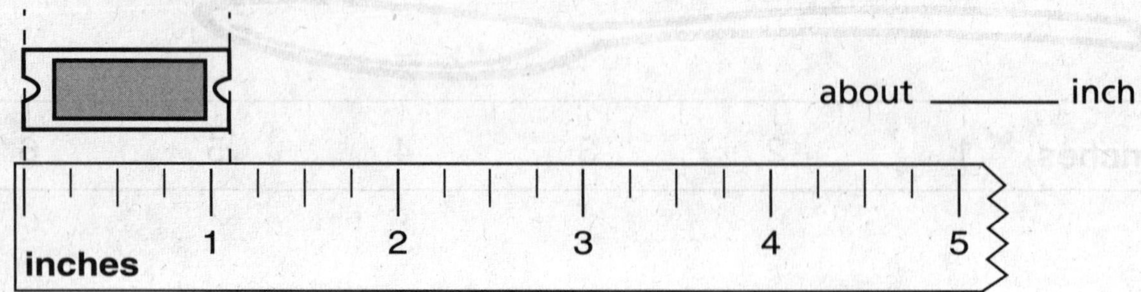

about ______ inch

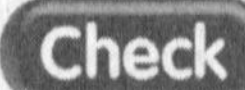

5. Draw a line that is about 3 inches long.

Name ____________________

Measure to the Nearest Inch

Skill 59

Learn the Math

Use an inch ruler to measure the length of an object to the nearest inch.

Vocabulary

inch
length

What is the length of the feather to the nearest inch?

Step 1 Line up the left end of the feather with the zero mark on the ruler.

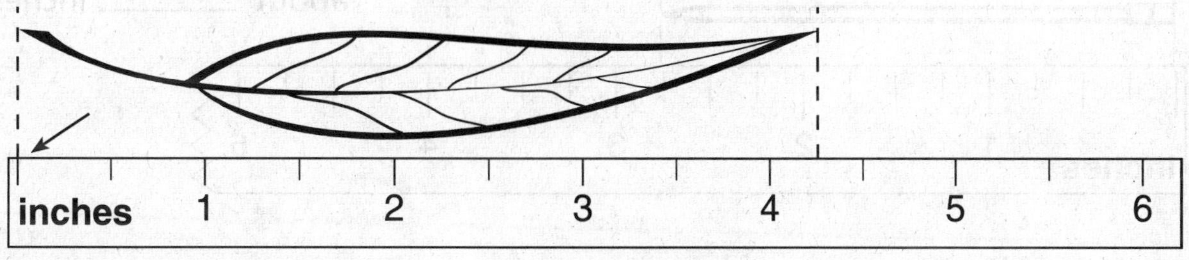

Step 2 Look at the right end of the feather. Which marks does it fall between?

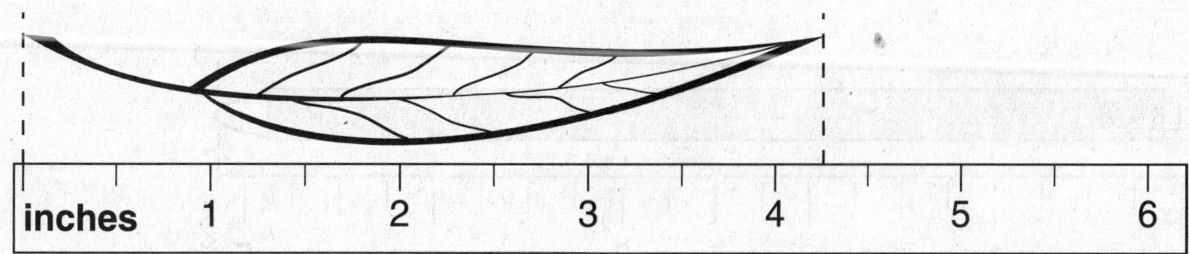

The right end of the feather is between the ____-inch and the ____-inch mark.

Step 3 Decide which inch mark the right end of the feather is closer to.

The right end of the feather is closer to the ____ -inch mark.

So, the feather is about ____ inches long.

Do the Math

Use an inch ruler. Measure the length to the nearest inch.

about ______ inches

1.

2.

about ______ inches

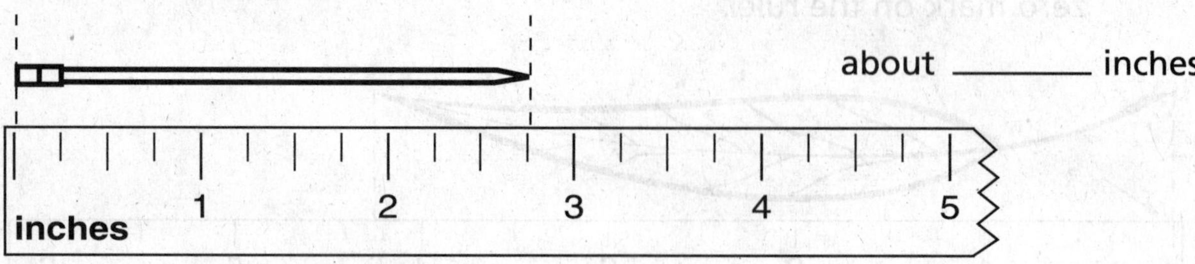

3.

about ______ inch

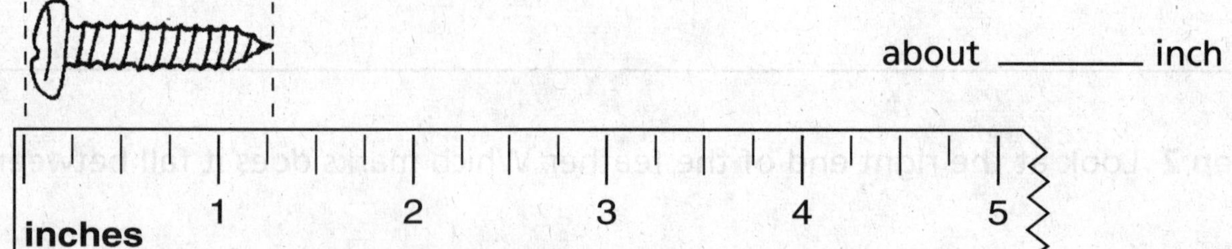

4.

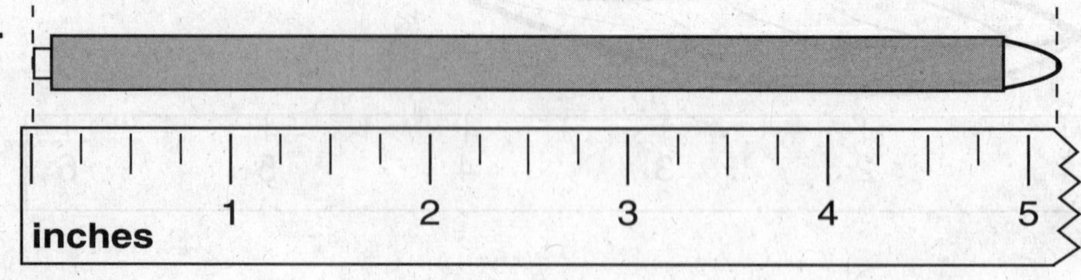

about ______ inches

Check

5. Look at Problem 2. Between which marks is the end of the toothpick? Explain why you would NOT say the toothpick is about 2 inches long.

____

____

____

Name____________________________________

Learn the Math

Weight is the measure of how heavy an object is.

Vocabulary

ounces
pound
weight

Use ounces to measure the weight of a light object.

A strawberry weighs about 1 ounce.

Use pounds to measure the weight of a heavier object.

A soccer ball weighs about 1 pound, or 16 ounces.

Choose the unit you would use to weigh a pencil. Write *ounce* or *pound*.

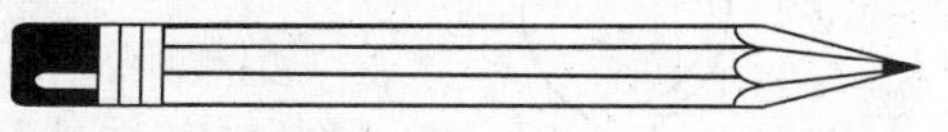

Think: A pencil feels lighter than a soccer ball.

So, you would use an ____________ to weigh a pencil.

Choose the unit you would use to weigh a chair. Write *ounce* or *pound*.

Think: A chair feels heavier than a soccer ball.

So, you would use a ____________ to weigh a chair.

Choose the unit you would use to weigh each. Write *ounce* or *pound*.

1. feather

____

2. lamp

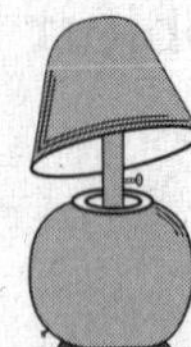

____

3. watermelon

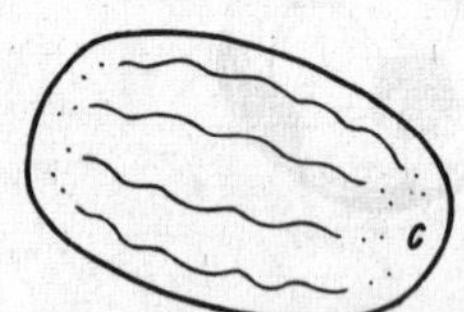

____

4. dollar bill

____

5. computer

____

6. balloon

____

Check

7. How can you estimate the actual weight of an object?

____

____

____

____

____

Name ____________________

Cups, Pints, Quarts, and Gallons

Skill 61

Learn the Math

Capacity is the amount a container can hold. Customary units used to measure capacity are cup (c), pint (pt), quart (qt), and gallon (gal).

Vocabulary

capacity
pint
cup
quart
gallon

cup (c)	pint (pt)	quart (qt)	gallon (gal)

Choose the unit you would use to measure the capacity of the cereal bowl. Write *cup, pint, quart*, or *gallon*.

Think: A cereal bowl can hold more than a cup, but less than a quart.

So, you would use a ____________ to measure the capacity of the cereal bowl.

Choose the unit you would use to measure the capacity of the bathtub. Write *cup, pint, quart*, or *gallon*.

Think: A bathtub can hold more than a cup, a pint, a quart, or a gallon.

So, you would use a ____________ to measure the capacity of a bathtub.

Do the Math

Choose the unit you would use to measure the capacity of each. Write *cup, pint, quart,* or *gallon*.

1. mug

____

2. pitcher

____

3. kitchen sink

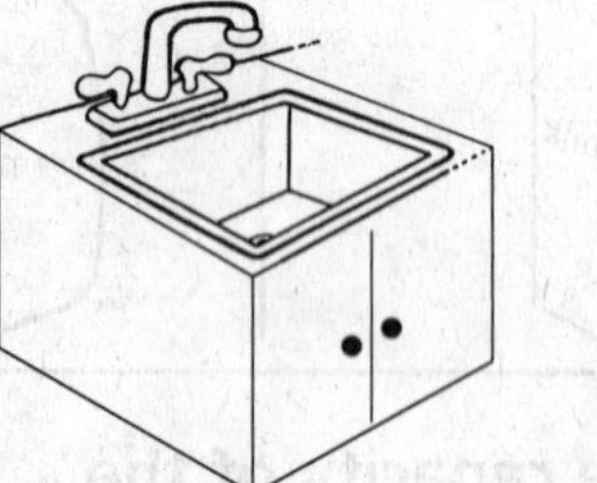

____

4. water bottle

____

5. flower pot

____

6. tea cup

____

7. How can you estimate the actual capacity of an object?

____

____

____

____

____

Name_______________________________________

Use a Metric Ruler

Skill 62

Learn the Math

Vocabulary

centimeter (cm)

You can use a centimeter ruler to measure how long an object is.

How long is the crayon?

Step 1 Line up the left end of the crayon with the 0 mark on the ruler.

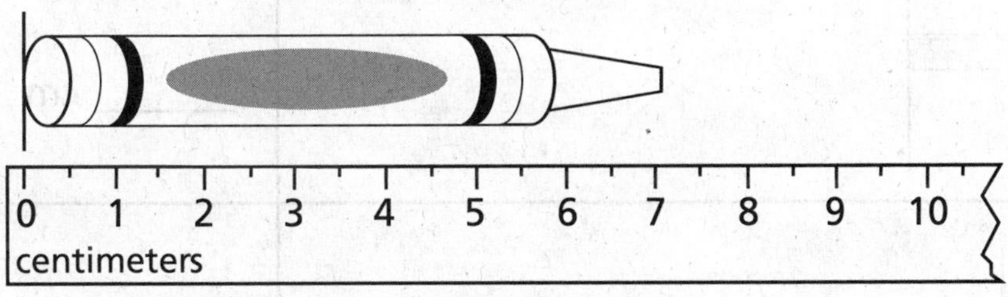

Step 2 Line up the right end of the crayon.

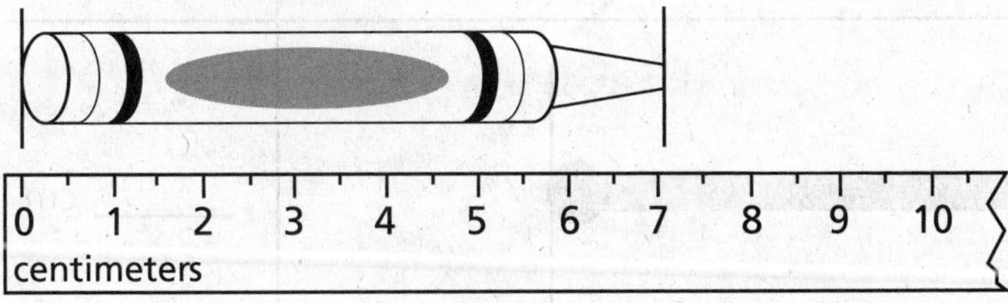

Step 3 What number lines up with the right end of the crayon?

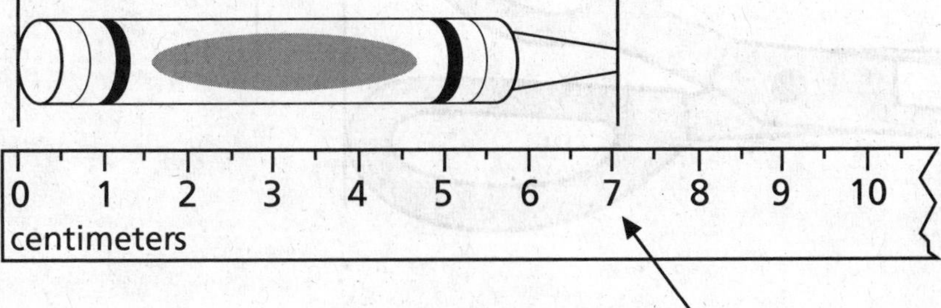

So, the crayon is____cm long.

Do the Math

Use a centimeter ruler to measure. Find the length in centimeters.

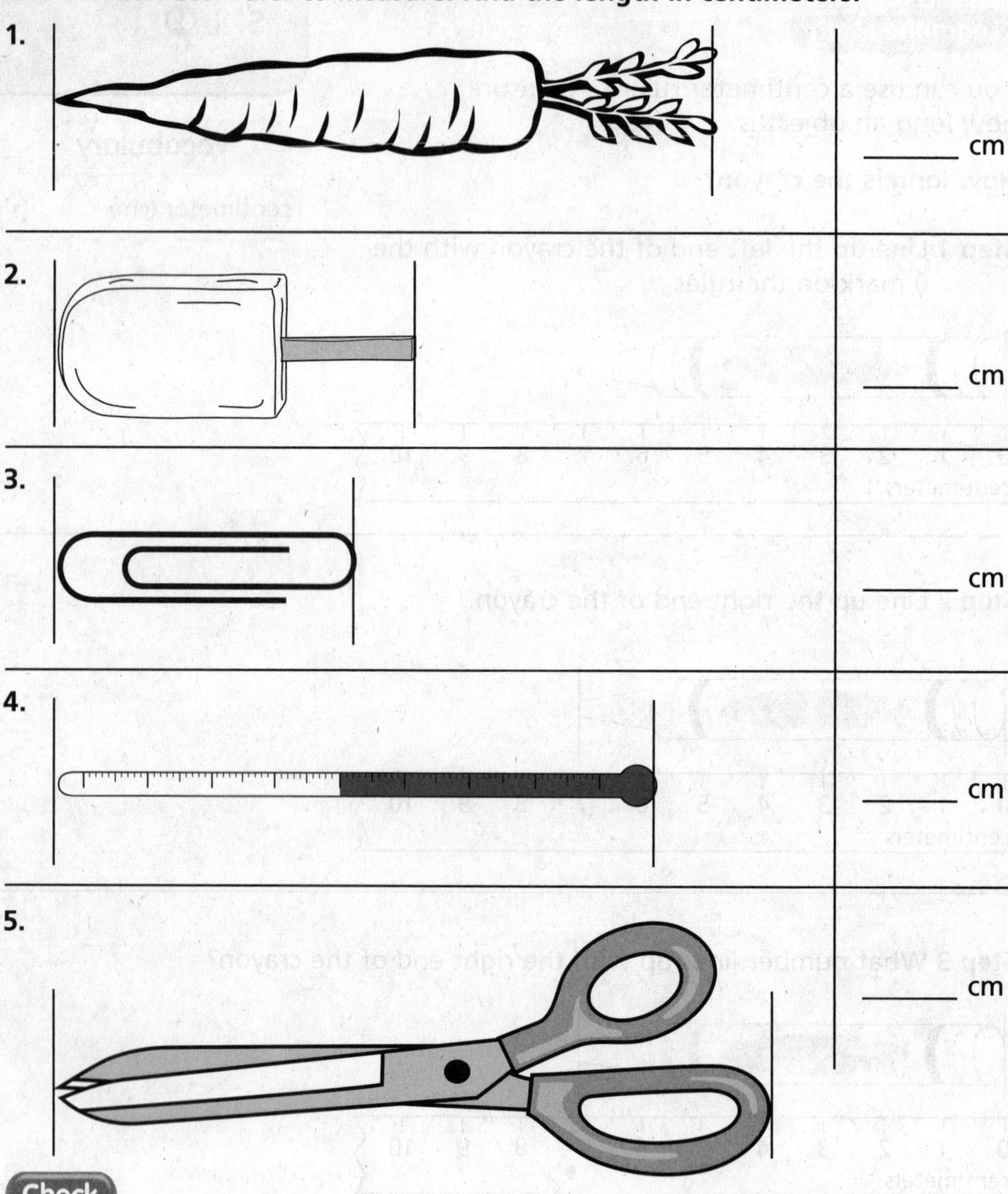

1. ______ cm

2. ______ cm

3. ______ cm

4. ______ cm

5. ______ cm

Check

6. Draw an object 3 cm long.

Name____

Measure to the Nearest Centimeter

Skill 63

Vocabulary

centimeter (cm)

Learn the Math

What is the length of the chalk to the nearest centimeter?

Step 1 Line up the left end of the chalk with the 0 mark on the ruler.

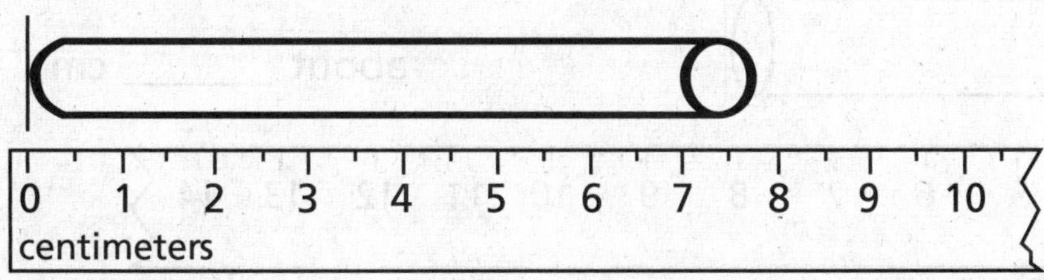

Step 2 Look at the right end of the chalk. What two centimeter marks is it between?

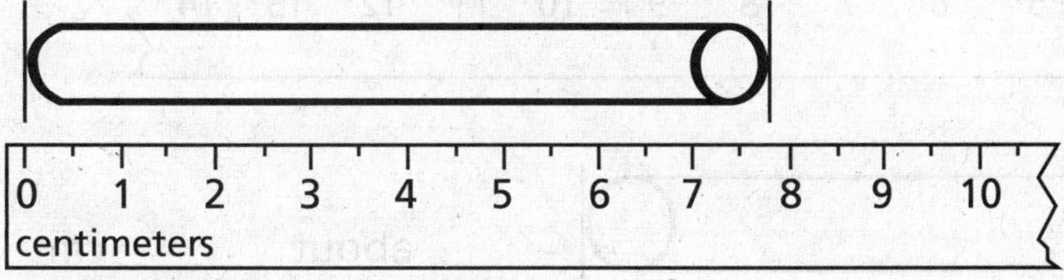

The right end of the chalk is between the

_______ -centimeter mark and the _______ -centimeter mark.

Step 3 Decide which centimeter mark the right end of the chalk is closer to.

The right end of the chalk is closer to the _______ -centimeter mark.

So, the chalk is about _______ centimeters long.

Find the length of the chalk to the nearest centimeter.

1.

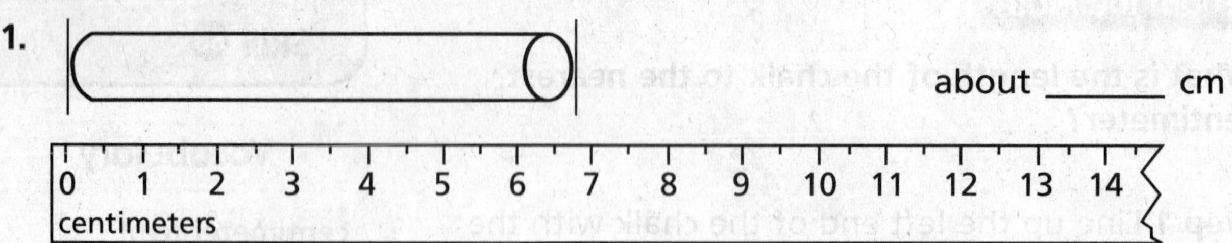

about ______ cm

2.

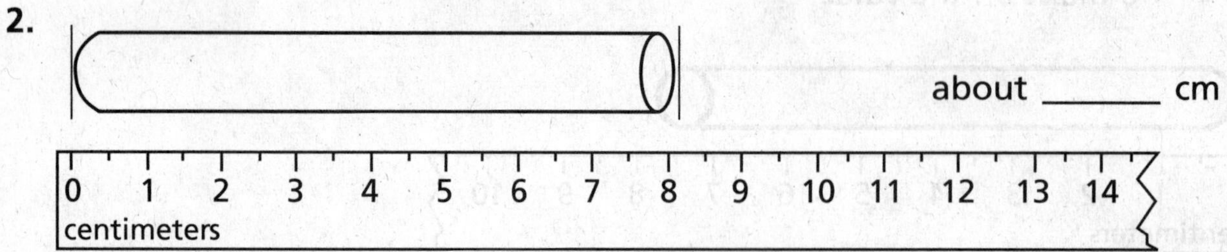

about ______ cm

3.

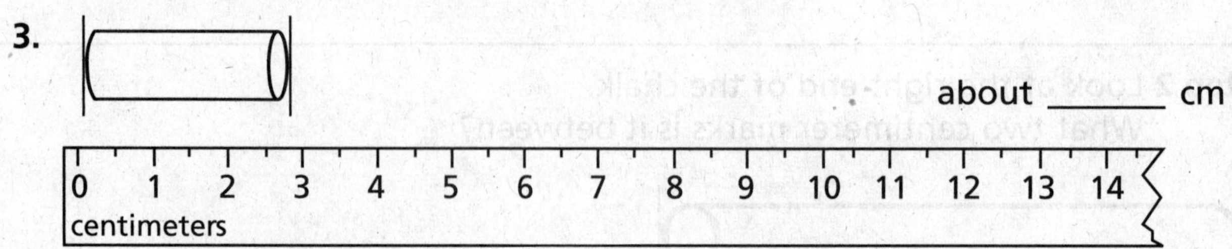

about ______ cm

4.

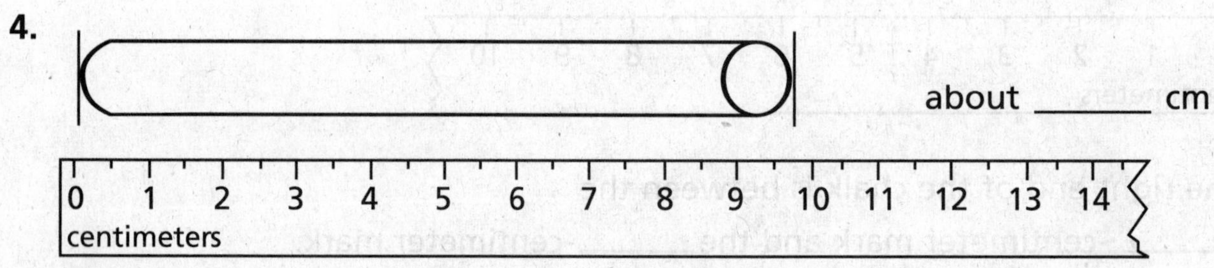

about ______ cm

Check

5. Draw a line that is about 6 cm long.

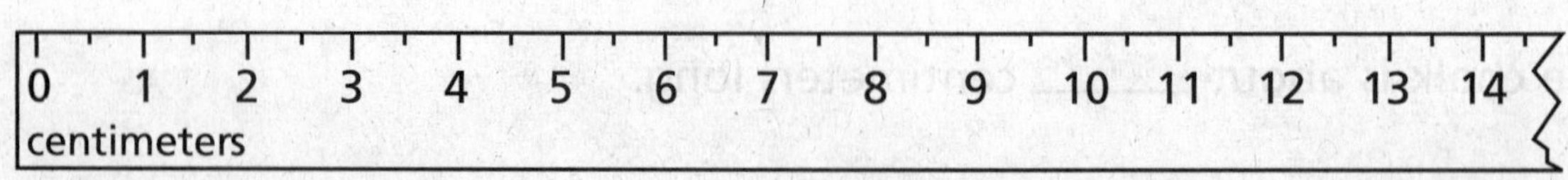

Name ____________________

Grams and Kilograms

Skill 64

Learn the Math

Mass is the amount of matter in an object.

Vocabulary

gram
kilogram
mass

Use grams to measure the mass of a light object.

A paper clip has a mass of about 1 gram.

Use kilograms to measure the mass of a heavier object.

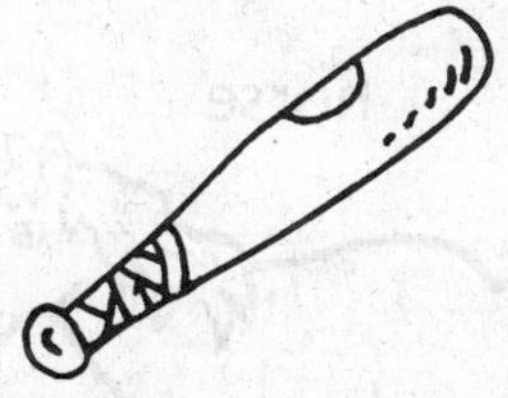

A baseball bat has the mass of about 1 kilogram.

Choose the unit you would use to find the mass of a quarter. Write *grams* or *kilograms*.

Think: A quarter has a mass less than a baseball bat.

So, you would use a ______________ to find the mass of a quarter.

Choose the unit you would use to find the mass of a dog. Write *gram* or *kilogram*.

Think: A dog has a mass more than a baseball bat.

So, you would use a ______________ to find the mass of a dog.

Choose the unit you would use to find the mass of each object. Write *gram* or *kilogram*.

1. scissors

____

2. cash register

____

3. horse

____

4. crayon

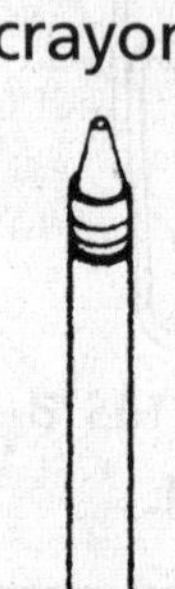

____

5. computer

____

6. bicycle

____

Check

7. Look at Problem 3. How can you estimate the actual mass of an object?

____

____

____

Name______________________________________

Milliliters and Liters

Skill 65

Learn the Math

Capacity is the amount a container can hold. Metric units used to measure capacity are milliliter (mL) and liter (L).

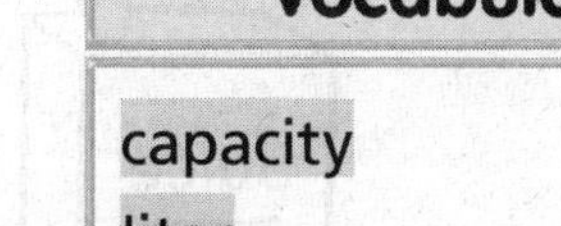

Vocabulary

capacity
liter
milliliter

A dropper holds about 1 milliliter.

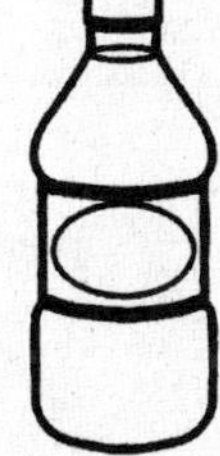

A water bottle holds about 1 liter.

Choose the unit you would use to measure the capacity of a spoon. Write *milliliter* or *liter*.

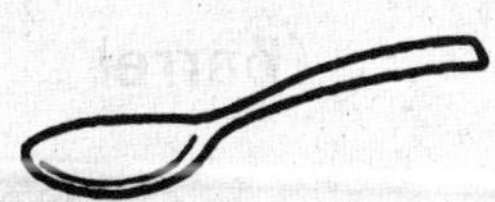

Think: A spoon can hold about the same amount as a dropper.

So, you would use a ______________ to measure the capacity of a spoon.

Choose the unit you would use to measure the capacity of a pail. Write *milliliter* or *liter*.

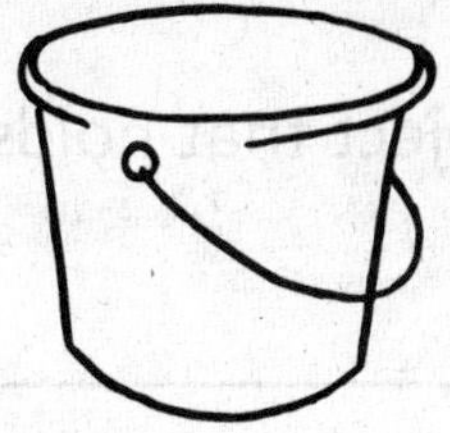

Think: A pail can hold more than a water bottle.

So, you would use a ______________ to measure the capacity of a pail.

Choose the unit you would use to measure the capacity of each. Write *milliliter* or *liter*.

1. juice box

____

2. cooking pot

____

3. fishtank

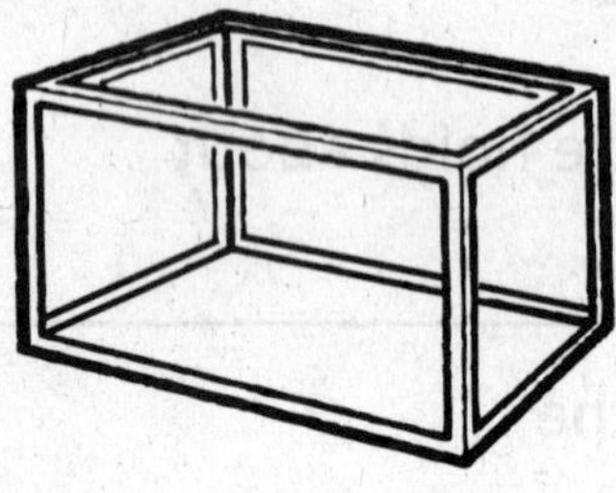

____

4. yogurt cup

____

5. pitcher

____

6. barrel

____

Check

7. How can you estimate the actual capacity of an object that holds more than a liter of liquid?

____

____

____

Name ______________________________

Column Addition

Skill 66

Vocabulary

addend
doubles

Learn the Math

You can group addends in any order to find the sum.

You can group addends to count on.

7	(7)	
2	(2)	
3	(3)	9
+ 6	+ (6)	+ 9
		18

You can look for addends to make a ten.

6	(6)	
4	(4)	10
2	2	2
+ 5	+ 5	+ 5
		17

You can look for doubles or doubles plus one.

6	(6)	
2	2	2
6	(6)	12
+ 1	+ 1	+ 1

Find the sum.

1. 3 + 5 + 7 + 5 = ____

2. 4 + 4 + 6 + 5 = ____

3. 3 + 4 + 7 + 2 = ____

4. 2 + 3 + 5 + 5 = ____

5. 5 + 6 + 1 + 2 = ____

6. 2 + 8 + 2 + 1 = ____

7. 3 + 5 + 2 + 1 = ____

8. 6 + 7 + 2 + 5 = ____

9. 8 + 2 + 4 + 4 = ____

Check

10. Look at Problem 6. How did you group the addends to solve the problem?

____

____

____

Name ____________________

Learn the Math

The distance around a figure is called the perimeter.

You can find the perimeter of a figure by adding the lengths of the sides.

Vocabulary

perimeter

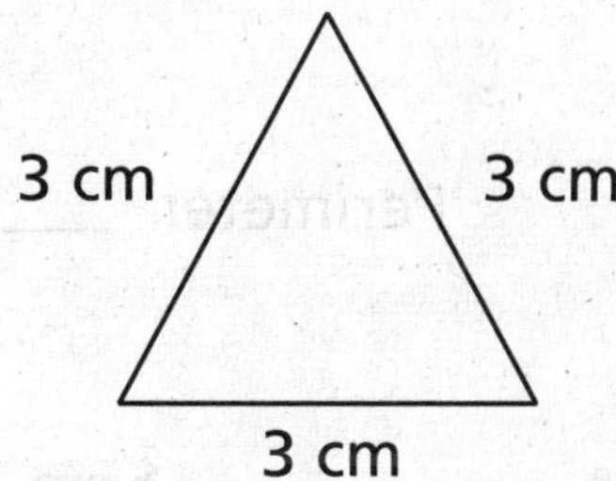

Remember

The abbreviation for centimeter is cm.

Add the lengths of the sides.

<u>3</u> cm + <u>3</u> cm + <u>3</u> cm = ___ cm

So, the perimeter is ___ centimeters.

Find the perimeter.

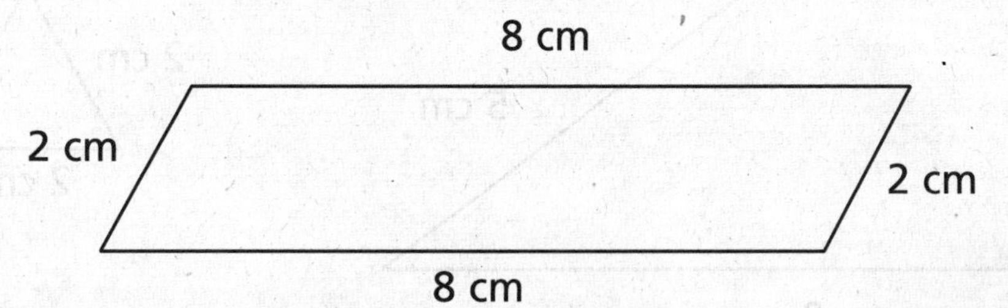

___ cm + ___ cm + ___ cm + ___ cm = ___ cm

So, the perimeter is ___ centimeters.

Find the perimeter.

1. 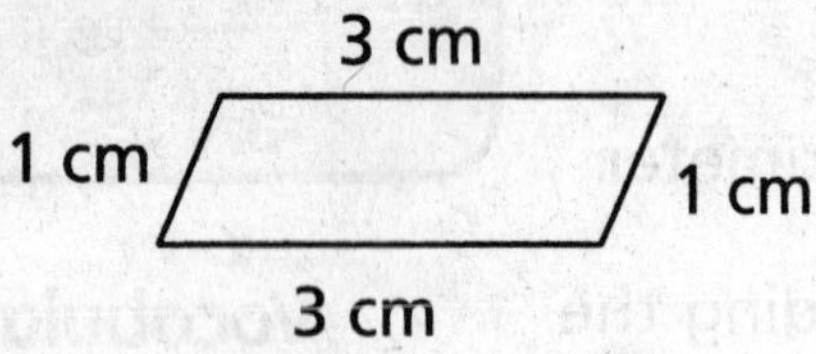

Perimeter _____ cm

2. 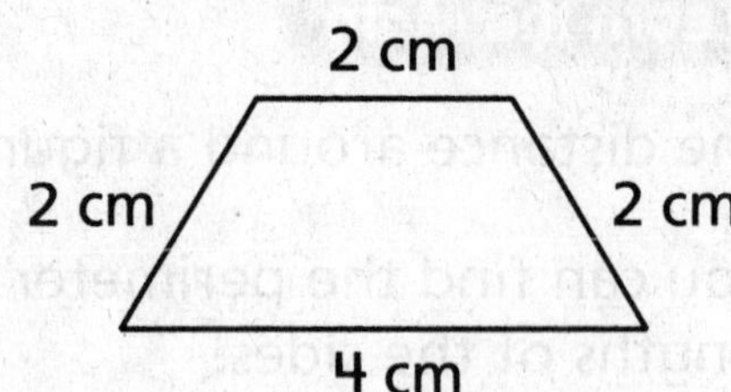

Perimeter _____ cm

3. 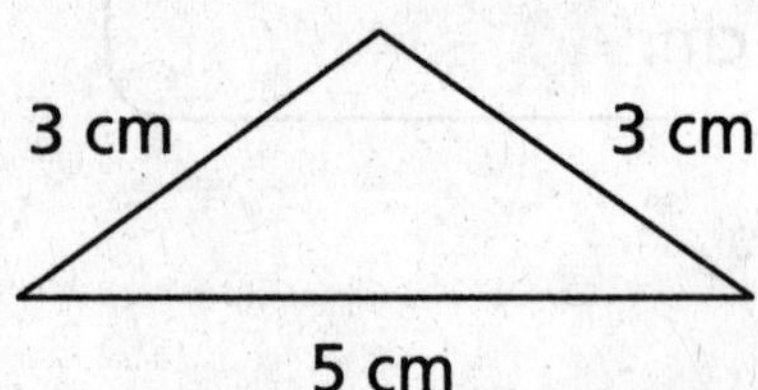

Perimeter _____ cm

4. 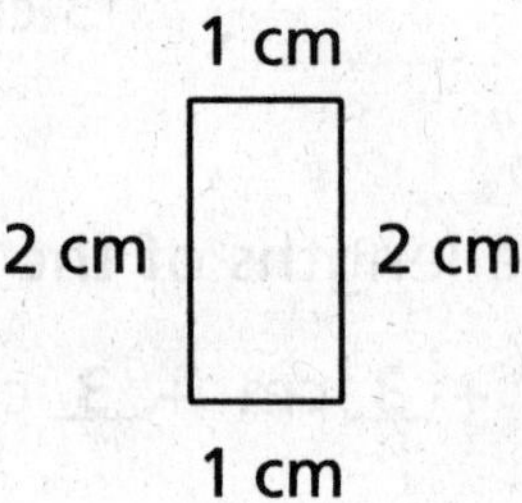

Perimeter _____ cm

5. 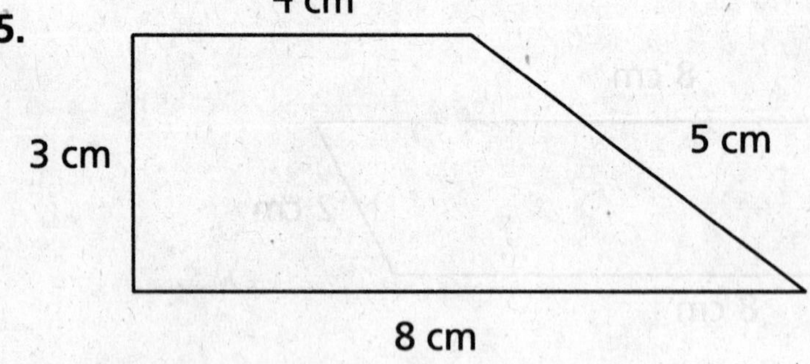

Perimeter __________

6. 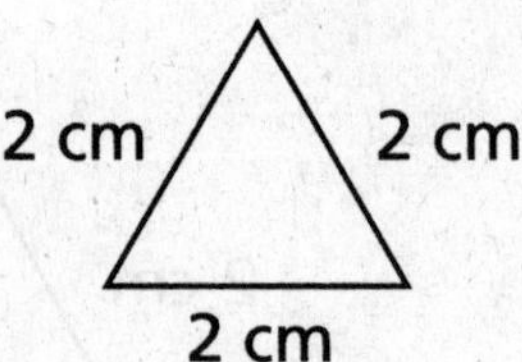

Perimeter __________

Check

7. Draw a rectangle with a perimeter of 12 cm. Label each side.

Name________________________________

Area

Skill 68

Learn the Math

Area is the number of square units needed to cover a flat surface. A square unit is a square with a side length of 1 unit.

Vocabulary

area
square unit

1 square unit

1 unit
1 unit | | 1 unit
1 unit

You count the number of square units to find area.

Count the square units to find the area of the large square.

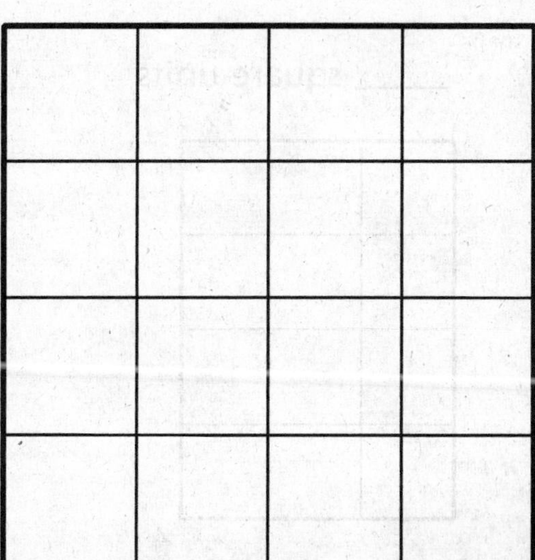

The area is ___ square units.

Count the square units to find the area of the rectangle.

The area is ___ square units.

Find the area of each figure.

1. 

_____ square units

2. 

_____ square units

3.

_____ square units

4. 

_____ square units

5. 

_____ square units

6. 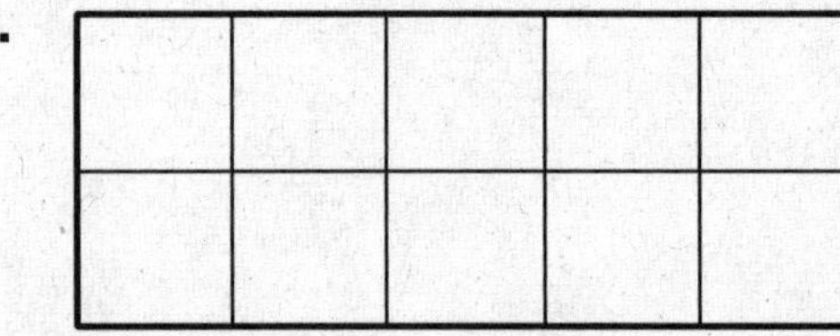

_____ square units

Check

7. Draw a square and a rectangle that each has an area of 16 square units.

Name________________________________

Length, Width, and Height

Skill 69

Learn the Math

Vocabulary

rectangular prism

A rectangular prism has length, width, and height.

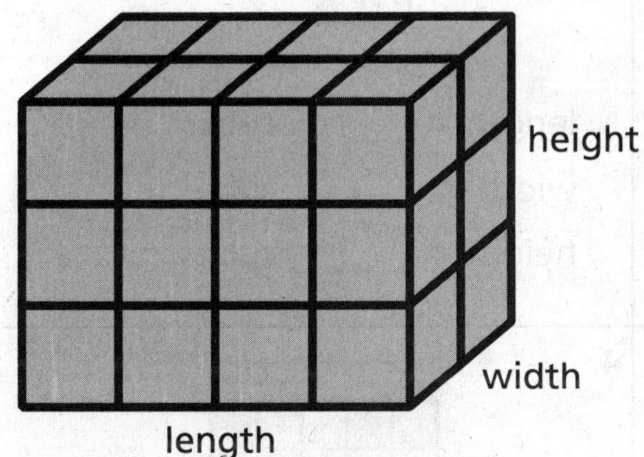

Count the cubes to find the length, width, and height.

The length is _______ cubes.	1 2 3 4 length
The width is _______ cubes.	2 1 width
The height is _______ cubes.	3 2 1 height

Do the Math

Count the cubes to find the length, width, and height of the rectangular prism.

1. 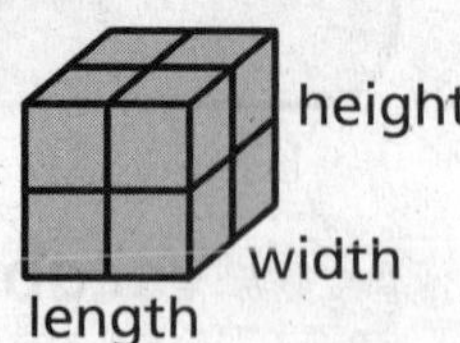

length = ______ cubes

width = ______ cubes

height = ______ cubes

2. 

length = ______ cubes

width = ______ cube

height = ______ cubes

3. 

length = ______ cubes

width = ______ cubes

height = ______ cubes

4. 

length = ______ cubes

width = ______ cubes

height = ______ cubes

5. 

length = ______ cubes

width = ______ cubes

height = ______ cubes

6. 

length = ______ cubes

width = ______ cubes

height = ______ cubes

Check

7. What are the length, width, and height of a single cube?

length = ______ cube

width = ______ cube

height = ______ cube

Name ______________________________

Explore Volume

Skill 70

Learn the Math

Volume is the amount of space a solid figure takes up. A cubic unit is used to measure volume. A cubic unit is a cube with a side length of 1 unit.

Vocabulary

cubic unit
volume

Find the volume of this solid.

One way to find the volume is to count and add.

1 cube

Step 1

Count the number of cubes in one layer. There are ____ cubes in one layer.

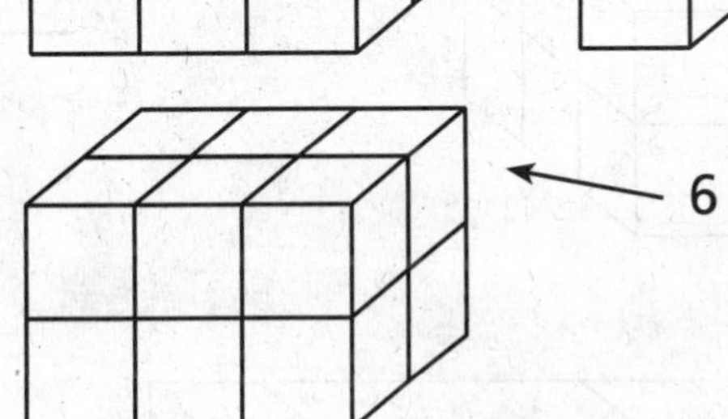

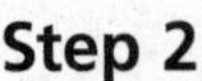

Step 2

Then add the numbers of cubes in each layer.

6 + 6 = ____

So, the volume is ____ cubic units.

Another way to find the volume of a solid is to count and multiply.

Step 1

Count the number of cubes in the top layer.

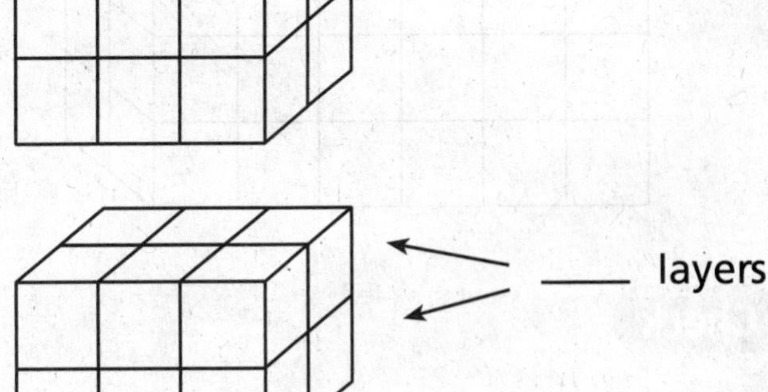

Step 2

Count the number of layers.

Step 3

Multiply the number of layers by the number of cubes in each layer.

2 layers × 6 cubes per layer =

____ cubic units

So, the volume is ____ cubic units.

Find the volume of each solid.

1.

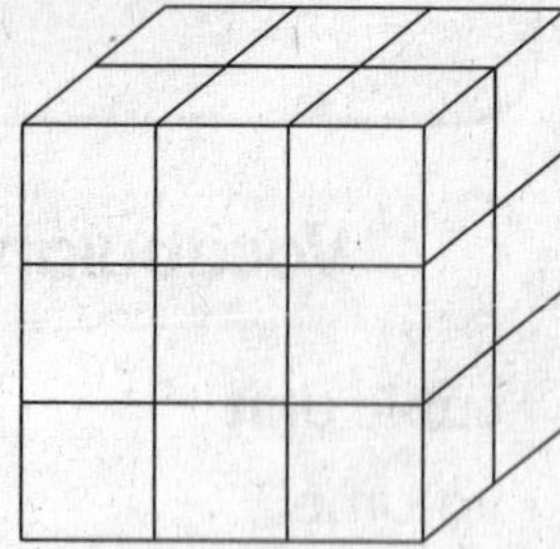

____ layers × ____ cubes per layer = ____ cubic units

2.

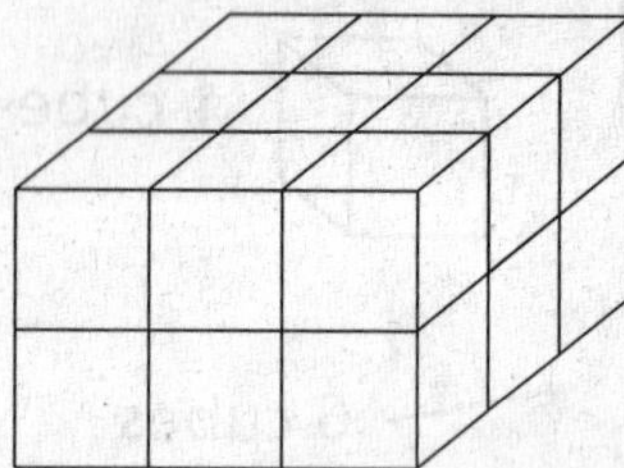

____ layers × ____ cubes per layer = ____ cubic units

3.

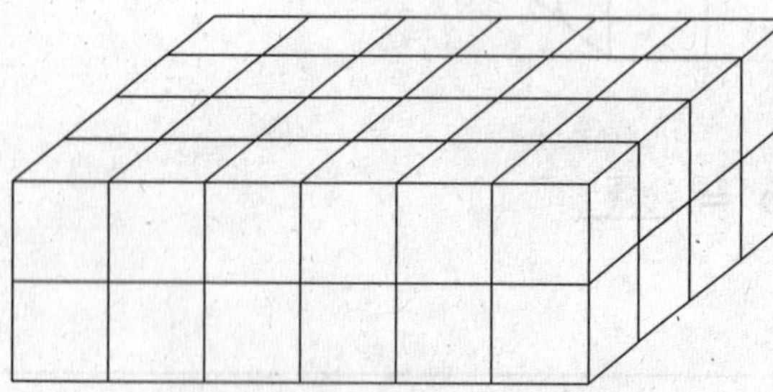

____ layers × ____ cubes per layer = ____ cubic units

4.

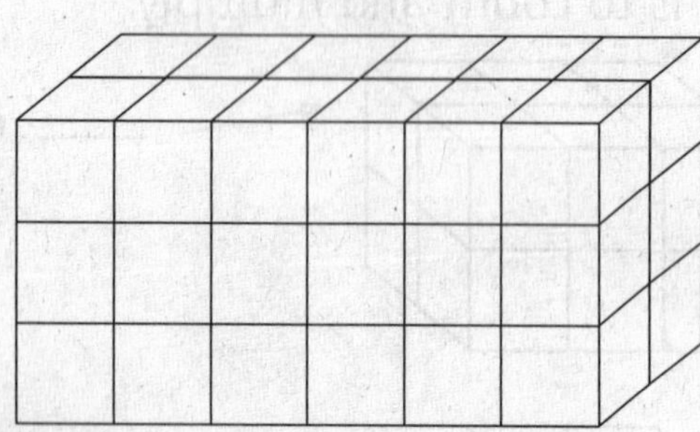

____ layers × ____ cubes per layer = ____ cubic units

Check

5. How can you find the volume of a box that can be filled with 2 layers of cubes where each layer is 4 cubes long and 2 cubes wide?

____

____

____